Implementing NetScaler VPX™
Second Edition

Implement the new features of Citrix NetScaler 11 to optimize and deploy secure web services on multiple virtualization platforms

Marius Sandbu

BIRMINGHAM - MUMBAI

Implementing NetScaler VPX™

Second Edition

Copyright © 2015 Packt Publishing

First published: October 2015

Production reference: 1161015

Published by Packt Publishing Ltd.
Livery Place
35 Livery Street
Birmingham B3 2PB, UK.

ISBN 978-1-78528-898-2

www.packtpub.com

Credits

Author
Marius Sandbu

Reviewer
Mikael Modin

Commissioning Editor
Priya Singh

Acquisition Editor
Harsha Bharwani

Content Development Editor
Riddhi Tuljapurkar

Technical Editor
Vivek Arora

Copy Editor
Puja Lalwani

Project Coordinator
Kinjal Bari

Proofreader
Safis Editing

Indexer
Tejal Soni

Graphics
Jason Monteiro

Production Coordinator
Manu Joseph

Cover Work
Manu Joseph

About the Author

Marius Sandbu is an IT architect, advisor, and trainer. He has worked with Microsoft technology for over 10 years and has been awarded an MVP title from Microsoft for his great dedication to the Microsoft community. He is also a board member of the local Microsoft technology user group and has spoken at many public events at Microsoft, Citrix, and other events. He has always had a strong interest in technology, and he also works as an instructor for Veeam and Citrix. Over the past few years, he has been awarded titles across different areas of technology, and he also had a role within Microsoft as an infrastructure ranger. He is a certified Microsoft trainer and has conducted different courses on System Center and Windows Server over the years. He is also an active blogger at `https://msandbu.wordpress.com/`.

> I would like to thank my wife, Silje, for supporting me and always telling me to pursue my projects; love you!

About the Reviewer

Mikael Modin is a Citrix certified instructor and senior consultant at Wedel IT, with over 15 years of experience working with Citrix and Microsoft technologies.

He is also a board member of Citrix User Group Norway and is an engaging speaker at Citrix-related events.

You can follow him on Twitter at `@mikael_modin` or contact him at `mikael@wedelit.no`.

Wedel IT is a consulting company based in Norway that specializes in virtualization technologies, primarily Citrix. The company was founded in 2010 and the employees are known for their expertise in the field and work with a range of customers both in the private and public sectors.

> I would like to thank my coworkers, who keep my days interesting, and especially my wife and kids, who are always there for me with their love and support.

www.PacktPub.com

Support files, eBooks, discount offers, and more

For support files and downloads related to your book, please visit www.PacktPub.com.

Did you know that Packt offers eBook versions of every book published, with PDF and ePub files available? You can upgrade to the eBook version at www.PacktPub.com and as a print book customer, you are entitled to a discount on the eBook copy. Get in touch with us at service@packtpub.com for more details.

At www.PacktPub.com, you can also read a collection of free technical articles, sign up for a range of free newsletters and receive exclusive discounts and offers on Packt books and eBooks.

https://www2.packtpub.com/books/subscription/packtlib

Do you need instant solutions to your IT questions? PacktLib is Packt's online digital book library. Here, you can search, access, and read Packt's entire library of books.

Why subscribe?

- Fully searchable across every book published by Packt
- Copy and paste, print, and bookmark content
- On demand and accessible via a web browser

Free access for Packt account holders

If you have an account with Packt at www.PacktPub.com, you can use this to access PacktLib today and view 9 entirely free books. Simply use your login credentials for immediate access.

Instant updates on new Packt books

Get notified! Find out when new books are published by following @PacktEnterprise on Twitter or the *Packt Enterprise* Facebook page.

Table of Contents

Preface

NetScaler is becoming more essential in many environments and is often crucial because of many of the services it offers. This book, which is about implementing NetScaler VPX, covers all the basics on how to get started with NetScaler VPX in a virtual environment and how to deliver highly available services and remote access to a Citrix environment.

It starts off with an easy introduction on what the product is, what it can offer, and how to perform an initial setup both on an on-premises deployment and using public cloud offerings.

Later, it moves on to some of the more advanced features, such as remote access against Citrix, different VPN features, and optimizing network services.

It also covers high availability features, such as active/passive HA, clustering, and how to load balance many of the commonly used platforms such as Exchange, SQL, Lync, and other Citrix components. It shows you how to secure services using application firewall and AAA.

What this book covers

Chapter 1, NetScaler VPXTM 11 – Basics and Setup, covers the initial setup of NetScaler VPX in a virtual environment and in public clouds, such as Azure and Amazon. It also describes the different deployment types, features, and settings and tells us what they can do.

Chapter 2, NetScaler Gateway ™, explains how to set up the NetScaler Gateway feature against a XenApp/XenDesktop environment. It also covers how to set up SSL-based VPN and how to use the Unified Gateway feature.

Chapter 3, *Load Balancing*, covers how to set up load balancing against generic web services as well as many of the most used platforms, such as Exchange, SharePoint, MSSQL, and other Citrix products.

Chapter 4, *Mobilestream*, explains how to set up and configure compression, caching, and frontend optimization on NetScaler in order to increase performance on websites.

Chapter 5, *Optimizing NetScaler Traffic*, explains the different features and techniques that we can use in order to optimize network traffic in a virtual environment, such as TCP profiles and HTTP/2.

Chapter 6, *High Availability*, explains the different high-availability features and how to configure them. It also covers a basic setup of GSLB.

Chapter 7, *Security and Troubleshooting*, covers the use of different security features in NetScaler, such as Application Firewall, HTTP DoS, and so on. It also gives you an overview of how to troubleshoot a NetScaler appliance.

Chapter 8, *AAA Application Traffic*, explains how to set up and configure the AAA feature in NetScaler and how to use it to provide secure authentication and authorization to web services.

What you need for this book

You can download a trial version of the NetScaler virtual appliance from Citrix at `https://secureportal.citrix.com/MyCitrix/login/EvalLand.aspx?download id=1857216&LandingFrom=1005`.

You should also have a virtual environment running either VMware, Citrix XenServer, or Hyper-V. If you do not have a virtual environment, you can test it out on a client hypervisor.

For instance, if you are using Windows 8.1/10, you can use Client Hyper-V, which is an add-on that needs to be added from **Programs and Features** under **Control Panel**.

You can also use the VMware player, which is available at `https://my.vmware.com/web/vmware/free#desktop_end_user_computing/vmware_player/6_0`.

Who this book is for

This book is intended for system administrators who are working with either Citrix or networking and who want to learn how to implement NetScaler VPX in a virtual environment for use with, for instance, remote access for Citrix environments and CVPN and to load balance different services.

Conventions

In this book, you will find a number of text styles that distinguish between different kinds of information. Here are some examples of these styles and an explanation of their meaning.

Code words in text, database table names, folder names, filenames, file extensions, pathnames, dummy URLs, user input, and Twitter handles are shown as follows: "Start by typing `shell`, and then change the directory to `tmp cd /tmp`."

A block of code is set as follows:

```
<add name="X-Frame-Options" value="deny" />
<add name="Content-Security-Policy" value="frame-ancestors 'none'" />
```

Any command-line input or output is written as follows:

```
set system user nsroot password
```

New terms and **important words** are shown in bold. Words that you see on the screen, for example, in menus or dialog boxes, appear in the text like this: "At the bottom, choose **Secure Access Only** and click on **OK**."

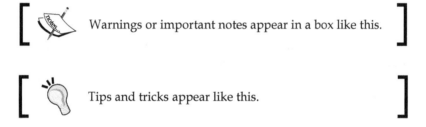

> Warnings or important notes appear in a box like this.

> Tips and tricks appear like this.

Reader feedback

Feedback from our readers is always welcome. Let us know what you think about this book—what you liked or disliked. Reader feedback is important for us as it helps us develop titles that you will really get the most out of.

To send us general feedback, simply e-mail feedback@packtpub.com, and mention the book's title in the subject of your message.

If there is a topic that you have expertise in and you are interested in either writing or contributing to a book, see our author guide at www.packtpub.com/authors.

Customer support

Now that you are the proud owner of a Packt book, we have a number of things to help you to get the most from your purchase.

Errata

Although we have taken every care to ensure the accuracy of our content, mistakes do happen. If you find a mistake in one of our books—maybe a mistake in the text or the code—we would be grateful if you could report this to us. By doing so, you can save other readers from frustration and help us improve subsequent versions of this book. If you find any errata, please report them by visiting `http://www.packtpub.com/submit-errata`, selecting your book, clicking on the **Errata Submission Form** link, and entering the details of your errata. Once your errata are verified, your submission will be accepted and the errata will be uploaded to our website or added to any list of existing errata under the Errata section of that title.

To view the previously submitted errata, go to `https://www.packtpub.com/books/content/support` and enter the name of the book in the search field. The required information will appear under the **Errata** section.

Piracy

Piracy of copyrighted material on the Internet is an ongoing problem across all media. At Packt, we take the protection of our copyright and licenses very seriously. If you come across any illegal copies of our works in any form on the Internet, please provide us with the location address or website name immediately so that we can pursue a remedy.

Please contact us at `copyright@packtpub.com` with a link to the suspected pirated material.

We appreciate your help in protecting our authors and our ability to bring you valuable content.

Questions

If you have a problem with any aspect of this book, you can contact us at `questions@packtpub.com`, and we will do our best to address the problem.

1
NetScaler VPX™ 11 – Basics and Setup

Welcome to the first chapter of the second edition of this book. Throughout the course of this book, we will cover most of the different areas where NetScaler serves its purpose. The first chapter will cover a short introduction of what Citrix NetScaler is and some of its features. Throughout this book, we will focus on how to set up and deploy a NetScaler VPX in a virtualized environment. The book will mostly show you how to set up and deploy in Hyper-V, but the process is not that different for vSphere and XenServer. I will also provide a short description on the deployment of NetScaler on public cloud providers such as Amazon and Azure.

So to sum it up, here's what we will cover throughout this chapter:

- Introduction to NetScaler and what's new in software version 11
- The definition of application delivery controller
- NetScaler gateway
- Differences between VPX, MPX, and SDX
- Editions and models
- Setup and configuring the basics
- Some deployment scenarios

Getting started with NetScaler®

NetScaler was an acquisition that Citrix made back in 2005, and it is one of the bestselling products in their portfolio today, pivotal in many large enterprises. Today, many of the largest IT organizations such as Microsoft, Google, and eBay, to mention a few, use NetScaler in front of their websites and services to ensure availability.

 We can check the kind of frontend solution an organization uses in most cases on their website by using a free web tool from http://www.netcraft.com/. For example, for eBay go to http://searchdns.netcraft.com/?restriction =site+contains&host=ebay.com.

NetScaler can be defined as a network appliance with the primary role of delivering services to end clients who connect to it. It does this by using different features, such as load balancing, high availability, gateway solutions, and so on. The commonly used term for it is **Application Delivery Controller** (**ADC**), as users in many cases connect to their services through, for example, a load-balanced web service such as NetScaler. It also has many features to optimize network traffic, such as web caching, compression, and SSL offloading, to give a service optimal performance. In addition, it includes features such as an application firewall, URL rewriting, frontend optimization, global server load balancing, and gateway function for XenApp/XenDesktop, to name a few. We will cover some of these features in greater detail in a later chapter.

So, NetScaler's whole purpose is to ensure that a service or an application is delivered through different availability and performance features. The following diagram presents some of the different uses of NetScaler and shows how users can access their different applications and services:

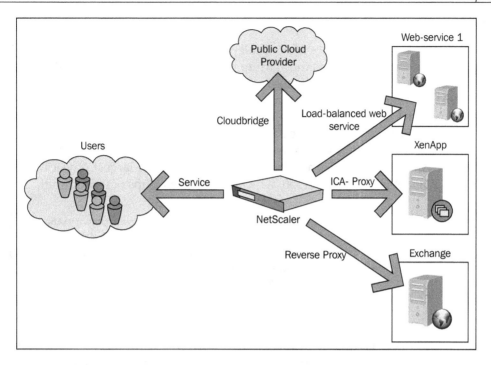

As we can see in the diagram, we can ensure content is delivered to users in many ways. Also, there are features that allow us to bridge different infrastructures, such as public cloud providers. We will delve into some of the features in the rest of the chapters.

NetScaler includes a variety of features; some information about the different features and the product itself can be found in the Citrix eDocs available at `http://support.citrix.com/proddocs/topic/netscaler/ns-gen-netscaler-wrapper-con.html`. eDocs is an ideal place for knowledge and support documentation about setup and configuration of the different features included in NetScaler.

NetScaler comes in three different flavors:

- MPX—Physical appliance
- SDX—Physical appliance with hypervisor capabilities
- VPX—Virtual appliance

MPX

The MPX is a physical appliance of NetScaler, which again comes in different models. As an example, the MPX 5550 is the starting platform that consists of an Intel CPU with 8 GB of RAM, and can handle up to 5,000 concurrent SSL VPN sessions and up to 175,000 HTTP requests every second. The MPX 5550 has a maximum throughput of 0.5 Gbps, but it can be upgraded to the 5650, which has 1 Gbps throughput. This only requires a change of license, as it still runs on the same hardware. A long list of different models that suit most business needs is available, depending on the number of users and the kind of service and bandwidth required. The largest physical appliance available is the MPX 21550, which has up to 50 Gbps of throughput.

 One of the benefits of NetScaler is that if we need better performance or more bandwidth, we can in many cases just upgrade the platform license to the next edition. You can refer to the NetScaler datasheet to see which platforms can be upgraded and check the specifications of the different platforms at http://www.citrix.com/content/ dam/citrix/en_us/documents/products-solutions/ netscaler-data-sheet.pdf.

All of the MPX models come with special SSL chips, which are specifically used to handle encrypted traffic (SSL traffic). NetScaler uses an architecture called nCore, which allows it to intelligently load balance the SSL operations among the chips available on the hardware. This allows for faster handling of SSL traffic on the platform. Also, an important point to remember is that each platform has a limit to the number of SSL-based operations and throughput it can handle each second, which can be viewed in the datasheet mentioned earlier.

SDX

The SDX is a special platform available on many of the same models as the MPX, as it uses the same underlying hardware. The difference is that the SDX itself cannot perform load balancing or any other NetScaler functions, as it is just a virtualization platform that runs a virtual NetScaler (VPX) on top of itself. By default, when purchasing an SDX, it ships with five VPXs. SDX runs a customized version of XenServer, and from there we can create multiple VPX instances running on top of it, which has all of the NetScaler features. This platform is better suited for multitenant environments; it is also suitable when we want to isolate the traffic into separate instances with dedicated bandwidth, VLANs, and/or applications.

Also important to remember is that when we have an SDX, we can have multiple VPX instances running — all with different software versions.

VPX

The VPX is available for XenServer, KVM, VMware, and Hyper-V, or as an instance on the SDX platform. The VPX can also be deployed on public cloud providers such as Microsoft Azure or Amazon Web Services.

There is a minor difference between running VPX in a regular virtual environment and as part of an SDX environment. In an SDX environment, the VPX has access to the onboard SSL chips and is able to handle SSL traffic accordingly. In a regular virtual environment, the VPX can handle only limited SSL traffic, as it is dependent on the virtualization host CPUs. Regular CPUs are not designed to handle SSL traffic as well as SSL chips; therefore, they have a soft limit on how many SSL connections they can handle. This can be seen in the NetScaler datasheet mentioned earlier.

Barry Schiffer has written an excellent article on NetScaler sizing and what model to choose, which I would recommend taking a look at if you are unsure of what to use. This article is available at `http://www.barryschiffer.com/citrix-NetScaler-platform-sizing-guide/`.

NetScaler also has different types of editions, and depending on the level, it will grant access to the different features. The three editions are Standard, Enterprise, and Platinum.

Standard is the most basic edition and contains most of the basic features, such as load balancing, SQL load balancing, NetScaler Gateway (formerly known as Access Gateway), network optimization, HTTP/URL rewrite, and more. The Enterprise edition gives us **Global Server Load Balancing (GSLB)**, HTTP compression, AAA management, frontend optimization and surge protection. Lastly, the Platinum edition gives us CloudBridge, full NetScaler Insight Center functionality, application firewall, and more. An important point to note here is that on an SDX appliance, all the VPX appliances have Platinum edition features.

There is also a dedicated Gateway instance that only has the NetScaler Gateway feature available. This only comes in a VPX 50 instance, which basically means that it has a 50 Mbps bandwidth limit and can only be used for Gateway features such as ICA-proxy, SSL VPN, or VPN. It is also available as a physical unit, the NetScaler Gateway MPX 500, which has the same limitations but up to a 500 Mbps bandwidth and a higher number of concurrent users.

Now, many of these features may be unfamiliar to you, but these will be covered throughout the later chapters.

> The complete feature set of NetScaler and its different editions can be found in the NetScaler datasheet available at `http://www.citrix.com/content/dam/citrix/en_us/documents/products-solutions/netscaler-data-sheet.pdf?accessmode=direct`.
>
> The datasheet for NetScaler Gateway can be found here `https://www.citrix.com/content/dam/citrix/en_us/documents/products-solutions/citrix-netscaler-gateway-secure-remote-access-from-anywhere-on-any-device.pdf`.

One of the things that I mentioned earlier was that in case we needed more bandwidth or better performance, we could just upgrade the license to another platform. The same goes for features as well; if we need features that are available in the Enterprise edition and we have only the Standard edition, we just have to buy a license upgrade to access those features. If, for example, we are in a situation where we need more bandwidth for a period of time, we can also purchase something called burst licenses. Burst licenses allow us to extend our bandwidth on the appliance, for example, for 90 days.

> There is also a free edition of the VPX called VPX Express. The VPX Express has the same functionality as VPX standard, but it has a limit of 5 Mbps of throughput and is valid for one year at a time. It also gives you access to running up to five users with NetScaler Gateway, which we will go through in the next chapter.

What is new in version 11?

Many may be familiar with the previous releases of NetScaler and some of its capabilities. Therefore, we decided to add what is new in version 11 of NetScaler OS. Version 11 was released in June 2015, and it introduced a bunch of new features and capabilities, including the following:

- Unified gateway
- Partition administration
- Media classification
- Jumbo frames support for VPX
- TCP Nile congestion algorithm
- Portal theme customization

- Web-front
- Authentication dashboard
- HTTP/2 support

Most of these topics will be covered throughout this book. If you wish for more information about version 11, you can read the release document at `https://www.citrix.com/content/dam/citrix/en_us/documents/ downloads/netscaler-adc/NS_11_55_20.html`.

Licensing

When we want to set up or deploy NetScaler, we need a license in place in order to access the features we want to use. An important point to note here is that three types of licenses are available for NetScaler:

- **Platform license**: This license is used for NetScaler to enable its different features, such as load balancing, content switching, and so on. It also defines the bandwidth.

- **Universal license**: This license is used for NetScaler Gateway features such as SSL VPN, CVPN, SmartAccess, and Endpoint analysis.

- **Feature license**: This license is used for features such as clustering, caching, compression, and so on. The specific features that can be bought as add-ons to an existing platform can be found in the datasheet.

 If you do not have access to a regular license, you can download a trial version of the latest NetScaler VPX Platinum edition from Citrix, available at `http://www.citrix.com/products/netscaler-application-delivery-controller/try.html`.

If you want to download a platform license for NetScaler from `https://www.citrix.com/`, you need to enter the MAC address of the first NIC on your appliance in the **Host ID** field on the website.

 If you are deploying a NetScaler Gateway VPX, and you want to download a platform license for it or generate universal licenses, both of these should be created with the hostname of the appliance instead of the MAC address. These licenses can be generated from the same website.

The MAC address can be found either via the CLI of the appliance or by using a hypervisor. We will look at CLI in detail in this chapter. To get hardware information from the CLI of the appliance, we have to first log in to the NetScaler System CLI, and then switch to the FreeBSD shell by typing `shell` and running the following command:

```
lmutil lmhostid
```

When using a hypervisor, such as the virtual machine manager PowerShell, run the following command:

```
Get-VM | Where { $_Name -match "VM" } | Get-SCNetworkAdapter | Select
MACAddress
```

If you are using VMware and have PowerCLI available, you can use a similar command as follows to get the same result:

```
Get-NetworkAdapter -VM NameofVM
```

This will give you the host ID/MAC address of the appliance, which needs to be entered on `https://www.citrix.com/` to generate a platform license. We will cover installing the license a little later.

Setup scenarios

When thinking about the deployment of NetScaler, a couple of things need to be taken into consideration:

- How is the network layout between the users and the service?
- What kind of network security is in place?
- Is the business using **Network Address Translation** (**NAT**) or any other kind of firewall that requires configuration to allow traffic?
- What service or application is going to be published?

A common scenario is load balancing some sort of a web service to external users. In such a scenario, a business might have a demilitarized zone and an intranet zone. One topology that can be used here is that NetScaler can be placed with one interface in the demilitarized zone and one interface in the intranet zone. This is also known as a two-armed setup. It is important to note that a two-armed setup is not necessarily two NICs connected to different networks; it may also be multiple VLANs trunked to the same NIC. This is practical for load balancing internal resources, as well because the traffic does not need to flow back and forth through the firewall multiple times.

In some cases, because of business requirements, you might have NetScaler attached to only one interface or only one VLAN that resides in the same zone. This is known as a one-armed setup. Here, NetScaler is placed, for example, in only the DMZ zone, and routing tables are in place to allow NetScaler to access the backend services. This type of topology emphasizes security. We will cover a sample scenario later in this chapter.

Now that we have gone through the different editions, features, and licensing, let us begin with the initial setup of NetScaler.

Creating our first setup

Before setting up the VPX, we need to make sure that we have the following resources available in our virtual environment:

- 2 GB RAM
- Two vCPUs
- 20 GB disk space

> NetScaler VPX supports a maximum of eight virtual network interfaces, and as of now, it supports Windows Server Hyper-V 2008 R2 and Windows Server Hyper-V 2012 R2. It also supports XenServer 6.0, XenServer 6.1, and VMware Vsphere from version 4.0 up to 5.5.

After downloading NetScaler from `www.mycitrix.com/`, we can import the virtual machine using the Hyper-V manager by selecting **Import Virtual Machine...** and browsing to the download location of NetScaler VPX.

After the appliance is imported, we should change the MAC address of the network adapter to static, as the license is based on the MAC address. Hyper-V manages MAC allocation for virtual machines, and in some scenarios, a virtual machine might generate a new MAC address. Therefore, it is important to set the MAC address as static.

This can be done by navigating to **Virtual Machine | Network | Advanced Features**, as shown in the following screenshot:

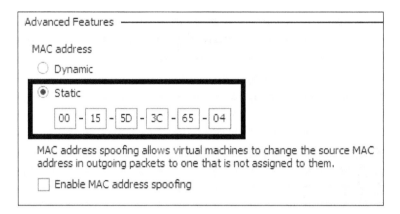

 Note that the same applies for VMware and XenServer as well.

After we are done changing the MAC address to static, we can boot the virtual appliance. The initial setup must be done using the CLI to connect the virtual machine console to the appliance console. The first thing we need to enter is the **NetScaler IP Address (NSIP)**, which is used for management purposes, then a subnet mask, and finally a default gateway. Now we can press 4 to save the settings. After this is done, we can then access the console using HTTP through the NSIP address that we entered earlier. The default username and password for the web administration GUI is nsroot and nsroot. Prior to logging in, make sure that the deployment type is set to NetScaler ADC. The management interface uses pure HTML 5, and it can be managed using any modern browser such as Internet Explorer, Google Chrome, or Firefox, for instance.

We also have the option of using SSH, so we can use any SSH-based client, such as Putty to perform management using CLI from there as well.

When logging in to the web console for the first time after the initial setup, we are presented with a wizard that allows us to enter information, such as DNS, time zone, and SNIP, and to change password settings. Alternatively, we can click on skip these tasks and go straight to the configuration dashboard. For the purpose of this book, I am going to show you how to add different configurations using regular GUI and CLI instead of using the built-in wizard. An important point to note here is that the initial setup wizard will always pop up until we have added a platform license, subnet IP, and NetScaler IP.

You can restart the initial setup in the CLI by typing the following command:

```
Configns
```

 When altering the configuration of NetScaler, the configurations are put into the running configuration file. If we do not save the configuration, the settings that we changed will be lost when we restart. Make sure to save the configuration using the CLI command save config, or by clicking on the **Save** button (represented as a floppy disk) in the GUI, after performing the changes to the configuration.

Deployment on Microsoft Azure

Microsoft and Citrix recently made NetScaler available as an appliance within Microsoft Azure, with a bring-your-own-license model, meaning that we can deploy a virtual appliance and use our own license there. However, we still need to pay Microsoft for the running instance and network traffic that is going out of Azure cloud. As of now, three versions are supported in Azure: VPX 10, VPX 200, and VPX 1000.

If we want to deploy a NetScaler VPX within Microsoft Azure, we have to use the current build available in the Microsoft Azure Marketplace. As of now, it is only available in the new management portal.

First, you need to have an active subscription in place for Microsoft Azure. Then, go to the new management portal at https://portal.azure.com.

Next, navigate to the marketplace, which can be found in the main menu, **Browse | Marketplace**.

Here, we type `Citrix NetScaler`, and it will appear in the list of options, as shown in the following screenshot:

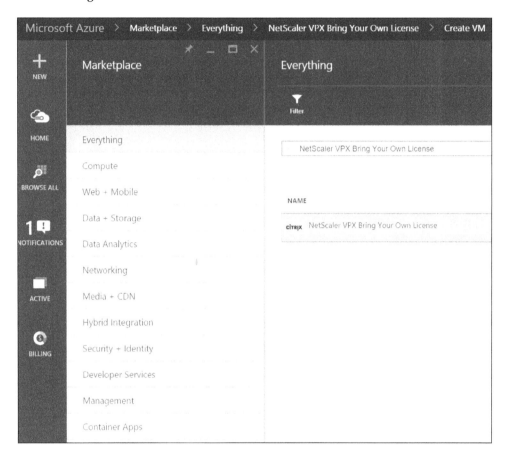

From there, click on **Create**. Then enter the required information, such as the IP address that will be used for management, username, and password. The default here is to enter `nsroot` and a custom password for that user. It is important to note that Microsoft Azure has its own DHCP service, which allows all virtual instances that run in Azure to get an IP address. Before deploying the virtual instance, you should define that the NetScaler VPX must use a static IP address to make sure that it does not lose its license in case of reboot or downtime, as in Azure, a virtual appliance may be moved to another and may be given another MAC address. In order to do so, navigate to **Optional Configuration | Network | IP ADDRESSES**. From here, you have the option to enter a static IP for the private IP address, which allows you to retain the IP address during reboots. Note also that Azure will automatically create a virtual network within a custom private IP range. So enter an IP address within the range that is created and click on **OK**.

The last thing to do before provisioning NetScaler is to enter a custom endpoint that will allow you to manage the appliance externally using HTTP. This can be done from within the provisioning wizard, before going into Optional Configuration. From here, you need to add an endpoint that defines which ports can be accessed externally. Here, add port 80 private, which is the internal port on NetScaler where management resides. Then, choose port TCP and then enter a public port. The public port nr will be used for external access later.

Another thing that is important to remember if you are deploying NetScaler in Azure is that by default, the appliance is deployed as an A2 Linux virtual machine. The A2 instance has a limitation of bandwidth of 200 Mbps. If you are planning to deploy a VPX 1000, you need to change this to an A4 instance.

NetScaler in Azure also has some additional limitations, for instance, it runs in a single-IP mode, meaning that we only have one useable IP address, so we use the same IP address for management, server traffic, and load balancing. As a part of this limitation, we can therefore not use the following ports for external services:

```
21, 22, 80, 443, 8080, 67, 161, 179, 500, 520, 3003, 3008, 3009,
3010, 3011, 4001, 5061, 9000, 7000
```

These ports cannot be used as they are used by the NetScaler for different purposes, such as high availability, management, and so on. Even though we cannot use these ports for our services on NetScaler, we can still use, for instance, 443 as an external port, since Azure has the concept of endpoints, which allow for port forwarding from one external port to another private port on NetScaler. Another thing to remember is that some features are not supported on NetScaler in Azure, which are: Clustering, IPv6, Gratuitous ARP (GARP), L2 Mode, Tagged VLAN, Dynamic Routing Virtual MAC (VMAC), USIP, GSLB, and CloudBridge Connector.

These features cannot be used because of the limitations of the network capabilities in Microsoft Azure. Also important is the fact that the current build running in the marketplace is the only one supported, so that means that we cannot do a direct upgrade as of now.

After we have deployed NetScaler in Azure, we access it using the FQDN given to us from the cloud service using SSH on a random port, or access it using HTTP on the custom endpoint we added.

By adding an HTTP-based endpoint against NetScaler in Azure, you are opening that port for all external users. You should, therefore, for security purposes, change the default password and add an endpoint ACL as soon as possible. You can also switch from HTTP to HTTPS-based traffic on the management IP. This also requires that you change the endpoint to 443 but allows for secure communication.

Deployment on Amazon Web Services

NetScaler is available as an Amazon Machine Image in the **Amazon Web Services** (**AWS**) marketplace, and like Azure, you need an active subscription to provision the virtual appliance. Head over to the management portal on `http://aws.amazon.com/` and choose login to the management portal. After logging in, you have the marketplace on the right-hand side, which, for reference, is located at `https://aws.amazon.com/marketplace`. Once there, search for `Citrix NetScaler` and press *Enter*. Now, you will get multiple options here as shown in the following screenshot:

You have the option to buy a finished Citrix licensed NetScaler appliance here, or you can buy an appliance without a license like with Azure. Choose the **Customer Licensed** option and then click on **Continue**.

Note that Citrix NetScaler in Amazon requires that you have a **virtual private cloud** (**VPC**) configured with three different subnets, which are not covered in this book. In order to learn how to configure VPC and different subnets, you can read more about it at `http://docs.aws.amazon.com/AmazonVPC/latest/UserGuide/VPC_Introduction.html`.

After the VPC and subnets are in place and the three different interfaces are placed within the three subnets, it's time to provision the virtual appliance.

Now, by default, the appliance will not get a public IP address attached to it, so you have to add an **elastic IP** address **(EIP)**.

This can be done through the EC2 dashboard by navigating to **Network and Security | Elastic IPs | Allocate New Address**. After allocating a new address, assign it to the management interface of the virtual appliance. Right-click on the address and choose **Associate Address**, then choose either **Instance** or **Network Interface** and find the management interface from the list. Then click on **Associate**.

After this, you can reach the NSIP using the EIP address on HTTP, as shown in the following screenshot:

To log in, use nsroot. The password will always be set to the instance ID, which can be seen from the EC2 dashboard as well.

As with Azure, there are some limitations to the deployment of NetScaler in Amazon, and some features are not supported, such as IPV6, **Gratuitous ARP (GARP)**, L2 mode, Tagged VLAN, and Dynamic Routing Virtual MAC (VMAC). However, unlike Azure, you are not bound to a single NIC and therefore do not have the same port restrictions.

Now, inside the main administration GUI we are presented with three main panes:

- **Dashboard**
- **Configuration**
- **Reporting**

Dashboard

The **Dashboard** pane gives us an overview of what is happening in NetScaler, how much CPU is used, how much memory is in use, what the throughput is, and so on. We can also view how many active sessions are using our services, such as load-balanced web services or VPN connections.

Reporting

We also have the **Reporting** pane, where we can run different built-in reports or create our own reports based upon different criteria. There are more than 100 built-in reports that we can use, for example, to see how many SSL connections have been used on the last day. We also have a link for documentation that redirects us to eDocs on Citrix, and a **Downloads** pane where we can download the SNMP MIB files, Nitro SDK, and some other files, such as integrations for System Center Operations Manager and Virtual Machine Manager.

The integration for Operations Manager allows for monitoring, and the integration for Virtual Machine Manager allows for fully automated deployment of load-balancing sets from within, for instance, a service template in Virtual Machine Manager. It also allows for automatic provisioning of more compute instance, for example, if NetScaler sees that servers that serve as load-balancing servers are running out of resources.

Configuration

The **Configuration** pane is where we do our configuration of services and also of NetScaler; this is where we will spend most of our time, and it also important how the GUI works and how to navigate in it.

By default, most of the features are disabled, which will appear in the GUI, as shown in the following screenshot:

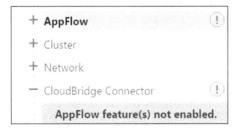

This is because if we do not need them running, NetScaler will not start the services that they depend on.

In order to enable a feature, we can right-click on it and choose enable. Alternatively, we can navigate to **System | Settings | Configure Modes**.

Most of the features are sorted by the tasks they do, for instance, content switching and frontend optimization are both optimization features and are placed within the Optimization menu. When working with the GUI, in most cases, we will see a plus sign, which indicates that more options are available or that we can add an option to an object:

In many cases, we want to edit existing objects. Most of the objects in this version allow us to do so by clicking on the pencil icon.

Many of the features contain nested options, so it is important to look at the navigation bar where, for instance, you might be adding a policy and attaching it to an action, as shown in the following screenshot:

Choose Type	Create NetScaler Gateway Session Policy	Create NetScaler Gateway Session Profile
Create NetScaler Gateway Session Profile		

Now, we configure some basic features before deploying any services to NetScaler:

- **DNS**: This feature allows for name resolution
- **NTP**: This feature allows for time synchronization
- **Syslog**: This feature allows for central logging of states, auditing, and status information
- **SNMP**: This feature allows NetScaler to send alarms to a designated SNMP server

Syslog and SNMP features are not needed but should be evaluated in larger deployments and for auditing and monitoring purposes. For example, NetScaler can be monitored using SNMP with System Center Operations Manager. You can read more about it at `http://msandbu.wordpress.com/2013/04/02/monitoring-netscaler-with-operations-manager-2012/`.

It can also be monitored using the NITRO API interface using, for instance, PowerShell or Comtrade management pack for Citrix NetScaler, which is an extension to Operations Manager.

The first to add is a DNS server to allow for name resolution. This setting can be found by navigating to **Configuration | Traffic Management | DNS | Name Servers**. Here, click on **Add** and enter the IP address of the DNS server, and leave the rest as default values. After you have added the DNS server, NetScaler will automatically start monitoring it. Make sure that ICMP is also opened in the firewall to the DNS servers; NetScaler uses ICMP with UDP to monitor if the DNS servers are available. For redundancy, you should add more than one DNS server to the list. After you have added the DNS servers, you can verify the state of the servers by going back to the **Name Servers** pane.

 DNS using TCP is only needed for zone transfers, and therefore it is not used for regular name resolution. We also have the ability to use both UDP and TCP. This is used for TCP-enabled DNS systems.

After each configuration, I am going to show the CLI-based option to perform the same action. To add a DNS server using the CLI, use the following command:

```
add dns nameServer IPaddress
```

Next, you should add an NTP server. This is important because of logging purposes, timestamps, certificates, reporting, and so on. The NTP server's configuration can be found by navigating to **System | NTP Servers**. Here, click on **Add** and enter the IP information and a key if you are using authentication. If you do not have an NTP server available in your network, you can use a public one. You can find a public NTP server at http://www.pool.ntp.org/en/.

You can also add an NTP server using the following command:

```
add ntp server IPaddress
```

After you have added the NTP server, you have to perform a sync using the following CLI command:

```
enable ntp sync
```

You also need to change the time zone of NetScaler to reflect your own time zone. This can be done by navigating to **System | Settings | Change time zone**.

Another important feature that you should look closer at is Syslog. Syslog is a common open standard logging feature that allows you to place logs on a central host instead of on NetScaler itself. This makes it easier to view logs from different devices that use Syslog from a single repository. This is not something that I consider as required, but it makes it easier to access and view logs.

If you do not set up Syslog, you will have to view the different logs locally on NetScaler. The Syslog feature can be enabled by navigating to **System** | **Auditing** | **Servers**. This requires that you have a central Syslog server in place.

If you have a central monitoring solution, you should consider configuring SNMP. SNMP consists of alarms and traps. If any abnormalities happen, such as high usage of RAM or, for example, Syslog, an alarm will trigger on NetScaler and the SNMP agent on it will send the alarm to an SNMP trap listener (which could be a central SNMP solution such as Microsoft System Center Operations Manager).

In order to allow NetScaler to be queried by an SNMP server for information, enter the following information, which can be added in the GUI by navigating to **System** | **SNMP**:

- **SNMP manager**: This is the IP address of the host that is allowed access
- **SNMP community string**: This is used for authentication of the appliance

In order for NetScaler to send traps whenever a critical event occurs, enter the following information:

- **Enable/Disable SNMP alarms**: This defines which alarms should create a trap
- **SNMP traps**: This defines which host should get the traps and the conditions for the traps

You can also change the hostname of the appliance, which by default comes with the name ns. You can change it using the following CLI command:

```
set ns hostname
```

Note that the hostname value you define here is used for licensing for the NetScaler Gateway VPX model.

You should also change the default password, as nsroot is the default password for all NetScaler appliances. This can be done using the following CLI command:

```
set system user nsroot password
```

This can also be done through the GUI by navigating to **System** | **User Administration** | **Users** | **nsroot** | **Choose Action** and clicking on **Change password**.

After you are done with this setup, you also need to add our platform license to the appliance. This can be done through the GUI by navigating to **System** | **Licenses**. Here, just click on **Add license** and upload the license that was generated from www.mycitrix.com/.

After adding the license, you need to reboot the appliance. You can verify that the license is properly applied by checking under the **Licenses** tab or by using the CLI command `show license`, as this will list all the features that are licensed along with the model type, as shown in the following screenshot:

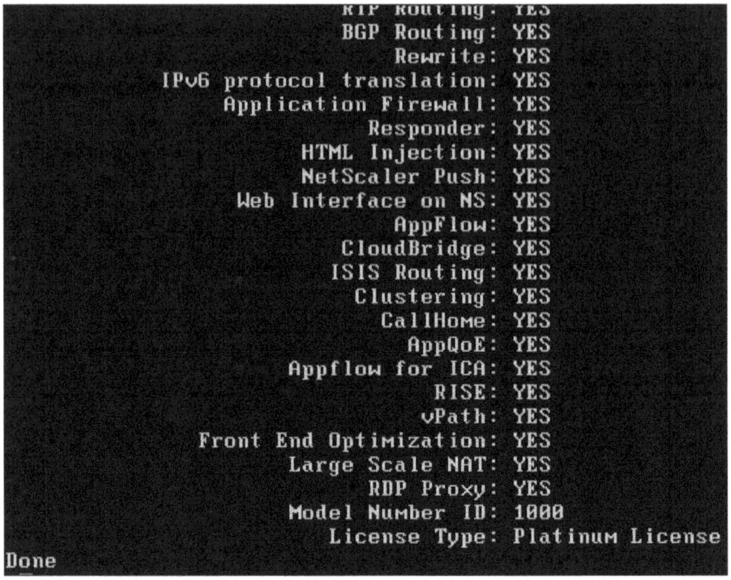

You can also see up in the top-left corner, which version of the VPX you are running from the number that is listed there.

Note that in the portal or CLI, if the model number ID is 1, it means that the license file has not been read correctly or the hostname allocation is wrong.

The last thing to do is to enable secure management of the NetScaler appliance, since by default, you can connect to it using telnet and regular HTTP, which is insecure. In order to set up secure access only, navigate to **System | Network | IPs** | Choose the NSIP and click on **Edit**. At the bottom, choose **Secure Access Only** and click on **OK**.

NetScaler® modes and features

Now that we have added the license and configured most of the basic features, such as DNS, NTP, and SNMP, it's time to take a closer look at the different modes through which NetScaler can process traffic. The different modes can be found by navigating to **System | Settings | Configure Modes**.

Here, there are modes that we can configure depending on the following parameters:

- How do we want NetScaler to process network traffic such as L2 and L3?
- Where is NetScaler placed?

Not all the advanced features are covered here, as some of them are not relevant for every environment. Information about the remaining features can be found in the Citrix article at `http://support.citrix.com/article/CTX121149`. The different modes here decide how NetScaler should handle different kinds of traffic. So, a quick overview of the different modes is as follows:

- **Fast Ramp**: This mode bypasses the slow-start mechanism of the TCP protocol and allows for a faster increment of TCP windowing, thereby allowing for faster packet transmission. This feature is enabled by default.

- **Layer 2 mode**: This mode allows NetScaler to behave as a switch and should only be used if servers are directly attached to NetScaler, or if it is being used as a transparent bridge, for example, CloudBridge.

- **Use Source IP**: By default, when NetScaler connects to a backend server, it uses one of its own addresses to establish a connection. By enabling the Use Source IP mode, the end client IP address is used to connect to the backend server. This should only be used in deployments where you need direct connections from the clients, or when you have an IDS environment. Make sure that when this feature is enabled, the backend servers must have one of NetScaler's IP addresses to be used as the Gateway IP address.

- **Client Keep-Alive**: This feature is mostly useful when the backend server or service does not support client keep-alive. It allows clients to maintain connectivity to the appliance even if the backend server closes the connection. This eliminates the need to reestablish the connection between the client and the backend server, and will reduce the time needed for a client to reopen the connection. This feature should only be enabled if there are performance issues with a service.

- **TCP Buffering**: This feature allows the adjustment of speed between a high-speed server and a slow client. If a backend server responds too fast for a client, the appliance will buffer the packets and adjust the speed based upon the speed of the client. This allows the backend server to devote the CPU resources to other tasks. This mode should be enabled if there are performance issues or if the TCP window scaling does not work, or shows high-packet loss.

- **MAC-based Forwarding**: This mode allows NetScaler to return packets based upon the MAC address of the received packet. For example, in environments where you have multiple routers, and you need to make sure that the packets are returned through the same path, you need to enable the MAC-based Forwarding mode. If this feature is disabled, the return path is based upon the route lookup. By default, this feature is not enabled.

- **Edge Configuration**: Enable this feature if clients are using the link load-balancing feature.

- **Use Subnet IP**: This feature allows for the use of subnet IP addresses.

- **Layer 3 mode**: When the Layer 3 mode is enabled, the NetScaler appliance performs route table lookups and forwards all packets that are not destined for any NetScaler-owned IP address. This mode is enabled by default, but it should be disabled if not used for security purposes.

- **Path MTU Discovery**: This mode allows network devices to share information to determine the largest MTU size that can be allowed on a network, which reduces the amount of IP packet fragmentation. This mode is enabled by default.

- **Static Route Advertisement**: This mode allows for the advertisement of static routes when using dynamic routing protocols.

- **Direct Route Advertisement**: This mode allows for the advertisement of direct routes when using dynamic routing protocols.

- **Intranet Route Advertisement**: This mode allows for the advertisement of intranet routes when using dynamic routing protocols.

- **IPv6 Static Route Advertisement**: This mode allows for the advertisement of IPv6 static routes when using dynamic routing protocols.

- **IPv6 Direct Route Advertisement**: This mode allows for the advertisement of IPv6 direct routes when using dynamic routing protocols.

- **Bridge BDPUs**: This mode is used for the Spanning Tree Protocol, allowing NetScaler to participate or not participate in the STP state.

- **Media Classification**: This mode is used to classify media content that is passed through NetScaler.

 When using NetScaler at the edge of the network as a firewall, uncheck all the boxes for route advertisement and Path MTU discovery.

NetScaler® networking

We have gone through the basic setup of NetScaler, its different modes, and its basic features. Now, we will go deeper into the different IP addresses that can be used in NetScaler and how they operate. NetScaler can have the following different IP addresses:

- **NSIP**: This is the NetScaler IP address
- **MIP**: This is the mapped IP address
- **SNIP**: This is the subnet IP address
- **VIP**: This is the virtual IP address
- **GSLBIP**: This is the Global Server Load Balancing site IP address
- **CLIP**: This is the cluster IP address

We will not cover clustering as part of this book.

NSIP

As we have discussed earlier, this IP address is used for management purposes in the local NetScaler, and it is used to authenticate against services such as AD, LDAP, and Radius. We need to make sure that the NSIP address is allowed to talk through the firewall.

By default, the NSIP address is allowed to be used for management services using several protocols, such as SSH, HTTP, and HTTPS. This is also the IP address we use to communicate with NetScaler using the NITRO API. We can restrict the security level to only allow secure access by navigating to **System | Network | IPs | NSIP**, and then choosing **Secure Access**. Remember that this requires that we import a trusted certificate, as by default, it uses a self-signed certificate. If we try to connect it with a browser when running a self-signed certificate, we will get browser warnings stating it cannot verify the publisher.

MIP

Next we have the MIP address, which is used for backend server connectivity. When we add an MIP address to a network, it automatically creates a route entry with its address as the gateway to reach that particular network.

SNIP

The SNIP address is also used for backend server connectivity. When setting up a NetScaler appliance, the startup wizard requires you to enter an SNIP address. The SNIP address also creates a route entry with its address as the gateway to reach that particular network. The SNIP address is also used for connectivity against DNS/WINS servers. In order to use an SNIP address, the **Use Subnet IP** (**USNIP**) feature must be enabled.

The common feature of both these addresses is that they are used for proxy connections by users connecting to a service via a VIP address to a backend server. Most of the time, MIP was used to set up an address on the same subnet in which the NSIP was placed, and the SNIP address was used to contact backend servers, which were located on another subnet. But with the latest releases of NetScaler, there is no need to use the MIP address feature. Citrix also recommends using SNIP instead of MIP addresses.

When we want to add an SNIP or an MIP address to NetScaler, we can do this from the same pane where we saw the NSIP address, that is, by navigating to **System | Network | IP addresses | Add**. If we want, we can also use the following CLI command:

```
add ns ip 10.0.0.0 255.255.255.0 -type SNIP
```

We can change the type name depending on what we need. Valid parameters here are SNIP, VIP, MIP, and NSIP.

VIP is a virtual IP address. It represents a service or different services by an IP address, port, and a protocol, and depending on the configuration, it might be a load-balanced service. Clients connect to this IP address to access a service. We will have a detailed look at how the VIP address works in *Chapter 2, NetScaler Gateway™*, and *Chapter 3, Load Balancing*.

Now, let us tie this together to understand the concept of how NetScaler processes traffic for a service. In this example, we have a web service running on a couple of web servers located on our intranet subnet 10.0.0.x. We want this service to be accessible to our external users by using NetScaler. We will place it in the DMZ with a two-arm topology, with one NIC in the intranet, and define the different IP addresses to be used. In this example, we set up an SNIP with the address as 10.0.0.2, which is used for server connectivity at the backend. Our users are placed on the Internet and will access the service using www.service1.company.com. This FQDN resolves into the VIP address on NetScaler, which is 80.80.80.80.

Remember that VIP is a virtual address, and in our example it is used to load balance the connection between the two web servers that are placed on the intranet, as shown in the following screenshot:

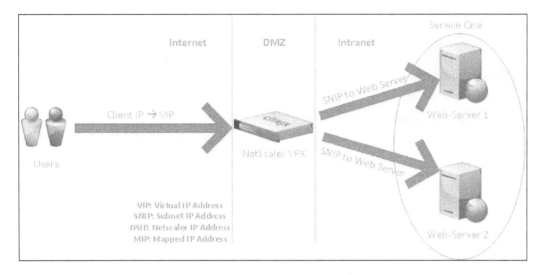

So, when a client connects to the VIP of NetScaler, it terminates the connection and establishes a connection with the backend web server using its SNIP client connection to the VIP address www.service1.company.com, as shown in the earlier example. The following table shows how the packets are routed:

HTTP request	Source	Destination
IP	Client IP address	NetScaler VIP address
MAC	Default router	NetScaler MAC

From here, NetScaler establishes a connection to the backend server on behalf of the client requesting the content.

HTTP request	Source	Destination
IP	NetScaler SNIP address	Backend web server 1
MAC	NetScaler MAC	Backend web server 1

The return traffic goes in the same direction back to the client.

This is a simple overview of how the traffic flow may be with a load-balanced service. There are, of course, many factors here that decide how the traffic flows, and it is also dependent on how the network is configured.

One thing that is important to note is that the IP addresses are not associated with an interface as they are with a regular network appliance. They are active on all the interfaces, so NetScaler behaves more like a hub. This might be a problem in some cases, where TCP packets are sent and received on different interfaces, and it might cause a loop. This is where VLANs come in. We can associate an IP address with a VLAN, which we can again associate with an interface. First, we need to create a VLAN. This can be done through the GUI by navigating to **Network | VLANs | Add**. From here, we can enter an ID for the VLAN and give it an alias name. Then, we can bind an interface and an IP address to the VLAN. This allows an IP address to be bound to a specific virtual interface.

We can also do this via the CLI by using the following commands. First, we need to create the VLAN as follows:

```
add vlan 20 -aliasName "Network 1"
```

Next, we need to bind it to an interface:

```
bind vlan 2 -ifnum 1/8
```

 We have an option to choose the Tagged VLAN. This uses the 802.1 standard, but it is not supported by NetScaler VPX, and it is recommended to leave this to the hypervisor layer. If we need to tag a particular VLAN to NetScaler, we can do this under the network settings for NetScaler VPX in the Hyper-V manager. To define a Tagged VLAN, enable the option for Virtual LAN Identification for a management operation system and define a VLAN ID.

Summary

We have now gone through the basics of NetScaler, covering the basics and the definition of an ADC, how it works, and also a bit on the different models and editions we can choose from. We also went through some advanced feature modes, and how NetScaler processes traffic for a sample web service. Lastly, we looked at how NetScaler handles traffic for a load-balanced service, and how we can add VLANs.

So, to sum it up, this is what we did to get NetScaler up and running:

- Imported the virtual machine in a virtual environment or in a public cloud
- Performed the initial setup of NetScaler using CLI by setting the NSIP
- Changed the default password from `nsroot`
- Added a platform license to enable more features

- Added additional IP addresses, such as SNIP, to enable backend communications
- Added a DNS server for name lookup and an NTP server for time synchronization
- Configured modes depending on the network topology
- Saved the configuration

In the next chapter, we will look more closely at the NetScaler Gateway and Unified Gateway feature, which is commonly used for XenApp/XenDesktop environments, and we will also have a look at the different modes it can operate in.

2
NetScaler Gateway™

NetScaler Gateway is one of the most commonly used features of NetScaler. In earlier versions, Citrix had products such as Secure Gateway or Access Gateway, but with the 10.1 release of NetScaler, it was renamed NetScaler Gateway. In the version 11 release, Citrix also introduced a new feature called Unified Gateway, which also builds upon the NetScaler Gateway feature. NetScaler Gateway does the same task that it did before; it grants users remote access through a gateway to the corporate network. It has multiple features and ways in which it can give end users access to the corporate network, which we will cover throughout this chapter. So here is a quick overview of what we will be covering in this chapter:

- Basics of NetScaler Gateway
- Different connection methods and settings
- Sample setup scenarios
- Integrating with XenDesktop/XenApp
- Configuring StoreFront
- Unified Gateway

Understanding the features of NetScaler Gateway

NetScaler Gateway has a set of features as follows, which can be used to grant end users remote access:

- **ICA Proxy**: This feature allows the gateway to proxy ICA traffic from the backend XenApp or XenDesktop solution to the user through the TCP 443 port.

- **SSL VPN**: This is a browser-based virtual private network (VPN) solution, which is also known as clientless access.

- **VPN**: This is a VPN feature that gives users access to the corporate network using the NetScaler Gateway plugin.

- **Endpoint analysis**: This is a network access control feature that scans clients to find out if they fulfill corporate security policy before they are allowed to connect to the network.

- **SmartAccess**: SmartAccess allows us to control access to applications and desktops on a server by using NetScaler session policies. You can read more about SmartAccess at `http://support.citrix.com/proddocs/topic/access-gateway-92/agee-smartaccess-how-it-works-c.html`.

- **MDX**: This is basically an application-level-based VPN solution used to integrate NetScaler with XenMobile application management.

The Gateway feature has more features, which we will cover as we go through the chapter. One important thing to note is that all of these features require that we have a legitimate license installed on our NetScaler. For the use of the regular ICA Proxy feature, we only need a regular platform license, which we covered in the previous chapter. If we want to use any of the other features in the preceding list, we will also need a license called the universal license, which is a concurrent user license.

When we purchase a regular NetScaler platform license, either for an MPX or for a VPX, we are given five universal licenses. We can verify this from the GUI by navigating to **System** | **Licenses**.

We can also verify this through the CLI using the following command:

```
show license
```

These licenses are concurrent, which means that we can have five users using a VPN-based solution at any given time. If we need more concurrent users, we will have to buy more universal licenses.

The most commonly used feature of NetScaler Gateway is ICA Proxy, which allows remote access for users to XenApp or XenDesktop solutions, and requires only that the users have Citrix Receiver installed. It requires no additional licenses. The solution is quite simple, as it tunnels all ICA traffic through the gateway and back to the user via port 443. This port is commonly used for secure HTTP traffic, is open on most firewalls, and is allowed at remote locations such as hotels and airports.

Let us take a look at a sample scenario to see how ICA Proxy operates and how a user can access their applications or desktops. This scenario describes an example, and it may differ from deployment to deployment depending on the network layout and infrastructure.

We have a company that has the NetScaler Gateway feature set up to allow remote users to access their XenApp solution. The example gateway is available at `https://login.company.com`, and the NSIP and SNIP are set up according to the design shown in the following figure:

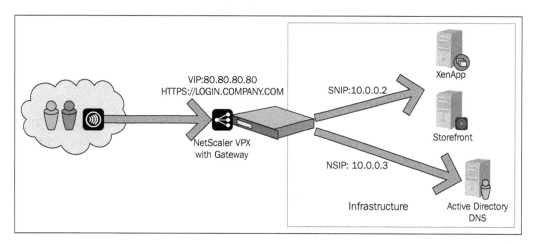

When a user tries to access the solution, for example, using the web portal, the following happens:

1. User 1 accesses the solution through `https://login.company.com`, which is accessible via the VIP on NetScaler.

2. User 1 authenticates his/her credentials on the site.

3. NetScaler uses its NSIP to contact the **Active Directory (AD)** to validate the user. If we have configured a load-balanced AD service, then it will use the SNIP.

4. The user is validated and the credentials are forwarded to the StoreFront Authentication service using the SNIP of NetScaler.

5. The StoreFront Authentication service forwards the credentials to the Store service, which in turn contacts the XenApp farm or XenDesktop controller using its XML service to validate the user against the STA and get a list of available resources.

6. The XML service from XenApp/XenDesktop contacts StoreFront and delivers a secure ticket and information regarding available resources.

7. The user is validated, and StoreFront contacts the callback URL to NetScaler using its FQDN. It then generates a list of resources available for the user.

Now, the user has a portal that shows all the available resources. If the user were to click on an application/desktop, the following would happen:

1. When User 1 clicks on **Application 1**, NetScaler sends an HTTPS request to the StoreFront server, which indicates which resource is being requested.

2. StoreFront connects to the XenApp farm using the XML service.

3. The STA service queries the IMA/FMA service for a resource that can launch **Application 1**.

4. The STA service returns a server that has available resources with its IP address to StoreFront.

5. StoreFront generates an ICA file, which contains the ticket issued by the STA and sends it to the client web browser. The ICA file that is generated contains the full FQDN name of the NetScaler Gateway VIP. The IP address of the backend server is never revealed as the resource is bound by the STA ticket.

6. Citrix Receiver launches a session with the FQDN and the STA ticket.

We have now seen how a sample scenario might look and how the different Citrix components communicate and generate an ICA connection with an external user. Even though we looked at how ICA Proxy operates, the procedure is not so different for a regular VPN connection.

Now, let us look closer at the configuration of the Gateway feature within NetScaler and see how we can set it up to reflect the sample scenario.

Deploying ICA Proxy

To deploy the ICA Proxy, we first need to enable the NetScaler Gateway feature. This can be done either in the GUI by navigating to **System | Settings | Configure Basic Features** and choosing **NetScaler Gateway** or by using the following CLI command:

```
enable ns feature SSLVPN
```

Starting with build 10.5, Citrix also introduced a quick wizard setup to integrate with XenApp and XenDesktop. This wizard is located further down on the left side under Configuration in the Management Interface, which will follow the same steps as we do throughout this chapter.

Then, we go into the NetScaler Gateway feature of the GUI. Here, we choose **Virtual Servers**, then right-click and choose **Add Server**. This will open a menu that allows us to create a virtual server that the clients are going to access.

Multiple configuration items are required in order to create a fully functional **virtual server (vServer)**. Remember that first we need to configure the default settings, such as NSIP, SNIP, and a functional license. Following are some of the settings we need to configure:

- **Name of the server**: This is purely for description purposes
- **IP Address**: This is going to be the VIP address
- **Port**: The default port is port 443

Then, we click on the **More** button to get access to the other configuration items within this feature. Here, we will get a list of different options that we can alter. We are not going to configure any of them except ICA Only. However, here's a short description of what each feature does:

- **RDP Server Profile**: This allows the NetScaler vServer to act as an RDS Gateway and proxy connection to RDP servers. We can also attach RDS shortcuts to the clientless access portal and allow users to connect to it using the vServer. This will be covered later in the chapter.
- **Maximum Users**: Here, we can specify how many concurrent users are allowed to log in to the vServer.
- **Max login attempts**: Here, we specify how many failed logins a user can have against a vServer.
- **Failed login timeout**: This specifies how long a user is locked out after exceeding the maximum login attempts.
- **Windows EPA Plugin Upgrade**: If the vServer should do a plugin upgrade for the EPA clients for Windows
- **Linux EPA Plugin Upgrade**: If the vServer should perform a plugin upgrade for the EPA clients for Linux.
- **Mac EPA Plugin Upgrade**: If the vServer should perform a plugin upgrade for the EPA clients for Mac.
- **Login Once**: This feature enables seamless SSO for the vServer, which eliminates the need for users to reauthenticate their credentials by, for instance, going from an SSL VPN–based vServer to an ICA Proxy vServer.
- **Double-hop**: This is needed if we have a double DMZ and the network traffic needs to traverse between two NetScaler appliances.

- **DTLS**: DTLS is a derivation of the SSL protocol that provides security services, but it is built upon the UDP protocol. This feature is used for services such as audio using UDP for ICA Proxy (`https://msandbu.wordpress.com/2015/03/16/enabling-citrix-receiver-audio-over-netscaler-gateway-with-dtls/`). It is also used Framehawk, which allows for better performance of ICA connections on high-latency WAN connections.

- **ICA Proxy Session Migration**: This feature is used to migrate an existing session from a user; when the user changes the device, their session is then migrated to that new device. This ensures that a user can only have one session at a time.

- **Enable Device Certificate**: This feature specifies if the vServer should check for device certificates as part of the Endpoint scan.

- **Enable Authentication**: This specifies if the vServer should authenticate. This will then trigger it to present a username and password dialog box to users trying to connect. If this is not enabled and the vServer is set to ICA Proxy, the users will be redirected to the web interface address.

- **Down State Flush**: Enabling this feature will allow the vServer to flush all new and existing connections if the vServer is set to disabled. If this feature is not enabled and we disable the vServer, all existing connections will be honored, but no new connections will occur.

- **Appflow Logging**: This feature is used to send AppFlow data to a collector, which is used for HDX data. This might be, for instance, Citrix NetScaler Insight for a third party such as Goliath for NetScaler.

- **ICA Only**: For configuration of ICA Proxy, we need to set this to ICA Only mode. If we uncheck this feature, it will be in SmartAccess mode. If we need an SSL VPN–based vServer, we should create another vServer and set it to SmartAccess mode.

We enter information such as **Name** and **IP Address** in the window:

Then, we click on the **More** button and set the vServer to ICA Only, leaving the rest at default for now, as shown in the following screenshot:

 This section assumes that you are familiar with how a digital certificate works, and what prerequisites are required to create one. In order to create a certificate, you first need a private key and a **Certificate Signing Request (CSR)**, which is sent to a third-party certificate issuer such as Go Daddy. In NetScaler, go to the **SSL** pane under **Traffic Management** in the GUI. This menu also allows you to import the certificate itself, along with the intermediate and root certificates. It also has an option to import PFX certificates, which often bundle the private key, the intermediate certificate, and the PFX certificate itself in one file. You can also use OpenSSL from NetScaler to convert a CRT certificate to a PFX certificate using the guide located at http://bit.ly/1lzMvEq.

The next step in setting up the vServer configuration is adding a digital certificate for the vServer. The typical way to do this is by going to the **Certificates** pane, clicking on **Server Certificate**, then clicking on the + sign and adding a certificate, as shown in the following screenshot:

This can either be installed from within NetScaler or fetched from a local drive on the device that is accessing the management interface. Now, depending on how the public certificate provider issues certificates, the steps may vary. Following are the cases:

- If we have a PFX certificate, it usually contains the private key, the intermediate certificate, and the PFX certificate itself. In this case, we need to choose PFX as the certificate filename and the private key filename. If the intermediate certificate is part of the file, we should also choose the certificate bundle.

- If we have a CER certificate, it usually contains a single certificate file and a key file, which contains the private key we need to add to it. If we have an additional intermediate certificate that we need to add to the vServer, we first have to import the certificate and choose **Add as CA**. In many cases, we may need to link the main certificate to an intermediate certificate to validate the chain. More information on how to configure it is available at `http://support.citrix.com/article/CTX114146`.

Derek Seaman has written an excellent blog describing how to add a certificate to NetScaler, which can be viewed at `http://www.derekseaman.com/2013/05/import-iis-ssl-certificate-to-citrix-netscaler.html`. Also, I have written a post on how to use OpenSSL to convert a CRT file to a PFX file. This can be viewed at `http://msandbu.wordpress.com/2012/10/15/convert-from-crt-to-pfx-with-openssl/`.

 Certificates that are imported into NetScaler are always stored under the `/nsconfig/ssl` folder.

After we have added a server certificate, we also need to add a CA certificate using the same steps. This certificate might be part of the PFX file for the server or may appear as a standalone CER file. After adding the CA certificate, click on **Continue**.

Now we need to add an authentication policy. There are two types of authentication policies: primary and secondary. The primary authentication type is typical LDAP (Active Directory), and the secondary might be a RADIUS solution for two-factor authentication. When the users try to log in, they will be presented with an interface that requires them to enter a username and password for the AD and a second password for the secondary authentication solution.

 NetScaler Gateway supports many methods of authentication, such as certificate-based authentication, SAML, WEB, DFA, SAML IDP. and even LOCAL users.

Now, this is largely dependent on how the RADIUS provider delivers the authentication process. An example is SafeNet, which we just need to add as a secondary RADIUS authentication provider. There are also others that completely replace the LDAP authentication process. I have provided links to different vendors and their setup for two-factor authentication. To set up RSA SecurEnvoy, follow the information available at `https://www.securenvoy.com/integrationguides/citrix%20net%20scaler%20with%20ipad.pdf`. For SafeNet, follow the guide at `http://www2.safenet-inc.com/sas/implementation-guides/Citrix/SAS-Citrix-Netscaler-Integartion-Guide-Rev-B.pdf`.

For mobile devices, such as iPad, we need to enter the RADIUS solution as the primary authentication. In order to sort the different authentication policies based upon which device is connecting, we need to use the appropriate expression. We are going to cover this later in the chapter. You can also read more about this at `http://support.citrix.com/article/CTX125364`.

As this scenario focuses only on single AD authentication, we only need to create a single primary authentication policy. Click on the **+** button under the **Authentication** pane. Then, from here, select **LDAP** under **Policy and Primary** as type. Click on **Continue**.

 If we want, it is also possible to allow users to change their AD password when accessing the Gateway using a web browser. This requires that the domain controllers are responding on LDAPS, and that the authentication policy is configured with the option to allow for password change.

Next, click on the **+** sign under **Select Policy**, since we need to assign a new policy to this vServer.

It is important that we understand how policies work in NetScaler before we continue, as this not only applies to authentication, but to other features in NetScaler as well. When we create a policy, we define an expression. An expression defines a statement that must be evaluated before a policy can be processed. For instance, we can define an expression based on whether a client is from a particular IP address. The expression is then based upon the statement allowed to process the policy. We can choose multiple options here. If we click on the **Expression Editor** button, we get numerous options that allow us to granularly define whom this policy should apply to.

In the following scenario, we want a policy to apply to all users who want to access this gateway. Therefore, we are going to add the `ns_true` expression, as shown in the following screenshot:

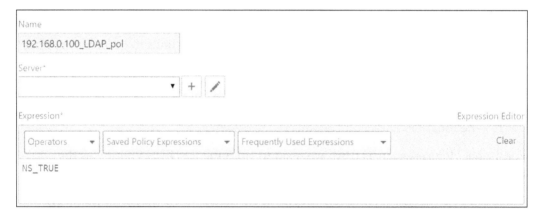

This expression can either be typed directly into the **Expression** field or found through the GUI under **Saved Policy Expressions**. The expression now states that this authentication policy should apply to all users that are connecting via NetScaler.

 You can read more about expressions and how to create sample expressions in the Citrix article at `http://support.citrix.com/proddocs/topic/ns-main-appexpert-10-map/ns-pi-config-classic-expr-tsk.html`.

After we have added the expression, we need to define a server that NetScaler can contact to verify the credentials. Under the **Server** pane, click on the **+** sign. Here, we need to enter information about the AD server, such as the following:

- **IP Address**: This is the IP address of the server.

- **Base DN**: This defines the organizational unit in AD where the users are located. For example, a base DN for an organizational unit called users in the domain `test.com` would look like `CN = users, DC = test, DC = com`.

- **Administrator Bind DN**: This is the username for an AD user who is allowed to query the domain. The username can be written in the domain/username form.

- **BindDN Password**: This is the password for the account and needs to be entered twice.

- **Server Log on Name Attribute**: This should be set to `samAccountName`. It is also possible to use `UserPrincipleName`. This allows users to log in with their e-mail addresses.

After this is done, you can check the connection to the domain controller and verify that the user has the correct rights by clicking on the **Retrieve Attributes** button.

 Using the Retrieve Attributes action does not initiate a connection from NetScaler itself to AD, but from the IP address of the machine that runs the browser that is connected to the NetScaler GUI.

Note that if we wanted to allow password changes for our users directly from the web portal, we would have had to change the security type to SSL/TLS and check the mark on **Allow Password Change** further down in the list.

Also, you might encounter a case where you would need the user to choose from different AD domains, for example, in a migration situation, or if you have multiple domains, from which the users need to choose a domain to log in to. By default, there is no built-in feature that allows users to choose from different domains. We can add multiple authentication policies that point to different domains, or we can use expressions to filter domains based upon different criteria, such as the IP address. We could also add a dropdown menu on the login portal that allows the users to choose from different domains. Citrix has published an article that covers how you can create a dropdown menu to choose a domain. You can read it at `http://support.citrix.com/article/CTX118657`.

However, note that you can use NetScaler in conjunction with cross-domains within the same forest as long as you point the LDAP policy to the Global Catalog port (`3268`), since the Global Catalog servers are the only ones that know of objects in other domains.

Also, in some cases, you might want to authenticate using UPN instead of samaccountname. The problem is that Storefront does not like UPN; therefore, we will need to alter the LDAP server configuration to accept userPrincipalName, as shown in the following screenshot:

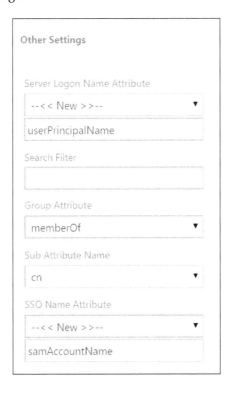

This will allow the NetScaler to authenticate the domain controller using the UPN. Then, it will forward samAccountName to the Storefront server.

If you are having issues with authentication from NetScaler to AD, you can use a built-in tool that can be run from the CLI. Start by typing shell, and then change the directory to tmp cd /tmp. Then run the following command:

cat aaad.debug

This will automatically generate events in the console for every authentication attempt. The task can be stopped by pressing *Ctrl* + *Z*. You can also view and see the status of your authentication attempts in the Authentication dashboard, which is shown as a separate feature in the menu on the left.

After we have finished adding an AD server, adding an expression, and naming the policy, we click on **Create**. This will then add the AD policy to the vServer. Notice that the policy has a priority of 0. If we have multiple policies here, the one with the lowest priority will win as long as the expression is the same. Therefore, if we were to have three primary authentication policies, all with the same configuration but with different priorities of 80, 90, and 100, and all trying to connect to the service, they would be bound to the policy that has the priority of 80.

Let us look at another example of how policies work. Suppose we have three authentication policies bound to a vServer, each with different priorities, and each of them has an expression that requires the client to have a particular IP address, such as the following:

- **Policy 1**: In this policy, the priority is 80. The expression is REQ.IP.SOURCEIP == 200.0.0.0 -net mask 255.0.0.0.

- **Policy 2**: In this policy, the priority is 90. The expression is REQ.IP.SOURCEIP == 210.0.0.0 -net mask 255.0.0.0.

- **Policy 3**: In this policy, the priority is 100. The expression is REQ.IP.SOURCEIP == 220.0.0.0 -net mask 255.0.0.0.

When a client connects, NetScaler will look at the list of policies, starting with the one with the lowest priority, and see if the clients match the criteria in the expression. If they do not match, it will go down the list until it gets a match. This is also the case if we have multiple RADIUS servers listed under secondary authentication. After adding the LDAP authentication policy, click on **Continue** to get the rest of the options available.

Now, the most important part that is needed to finish the configuration is the session policy. This can be found under **Policies**. Here, click on the + sign, and under **Choose Policy**, choose **Session** and click on **Continue**.

Now click on the **+** sign under **Select Policy**, since we need to create a new policy which will be assigned to this vServer in the same way as we did with the LDAP policy. We want all users to be bound to this policy, so we use the same general expression ns_true.

Next, we give this session policy a name and then add an action to the policy, which is a session profile. The session profile has information about where the StoreFront server is located, how it should forward credentials to the StoreFront server, whether ICA Proxy should be used, and so on.

Notice that we have the option to choose **Override Global** for every configuration item. Instead of defining settings at the vServer level, we can also define settings at a global level. Settings that are configured on a global level would then be the default for all vServers created in NetScaler. If we have settings set at a global level, and we wish to override these, we need to choose **Override Global**.

The **Network Configuration** pane has configurations used for regular VPN connections, which we will cover later in this chapter. Under the **Client Experience** pane, we have multiple settings that we need to configure. We are going to cover all of these, as some are used for ICA Proxy and some are used for SSL VPN or VPN. Following are the settings:

- **Home Page**: This is mostly used for XenMobile deployments and when you want to define a homepage for an SSL VPN session.

- **URL for Web-Based Email**: This is used for logging in to web-based e-mail solutions, such as Exchange OWA.

- **Split Tunnel**: This is used to define whether all client traffic or only traffic meant for destined servers in the network should go through the gateway in a VPN connection.

- **Session Time-out (mins)**: This defines how long NetScaler waits before it disconnects the session when there is no network traffic. This applies to all types of clients.

- **Client Idle Time-out (mins)**: This defines how long NetScaler waits before it disconnects the session when there is no user activity. This applies only to NetScaler plugins.

- **Clientless Access**: This defines whether the SSL-based VPN should be enabled or disabled.

- **Clientless Access URL Encoding**: This defines if the URLs of internal web applications are obscure or are in clear text and visible to the users.

- **Clientless Access Persistent Cookie**: This is needed for access to certain features in SharePoint, such as opening and editing documents.

- **Plug-in Type**: This defines what kind of plugin is offered to the user — whether it is Windows/Mac-based or Java-based.

- **Windows, Linux, and Mac plugins**: If the vServer is going to deliver updates to EPA clients.

- **Single Sign-on to Web Applications**: This allows NetScaler to perform SSO either for the web interface / StoreFront or for a custom homepage that is set to be the SharePoint site.

- **Credential Index**: This defines which authentication credentials are forwarded to the web application. Here, we can choose from the primary or the secondary authentication set.

- **KCD account**: This allows NetScaler to perform Kerberos-based authentication using a Kerberos constrained delegation (KCD) service account.

- **Single Sign-on with Windows**: This allows the Gateway plugin to authenticate to NetScaler using the Windows credentials.

- **Client Cleanup Prompt**: This is used to control the display of the client cleanup prompt after exiting an SSL VPN session. This feature is available for regular Windows-/Mac-based clients, but not for mobile devices.

We also have more features under the **Advanced Settings** pane, but they are not covered in this book.

All we need to do in the **Client Experience** pane is check the **Single Sign-on to Web Applications** option and set the **Credential Index** field to PRIMARY. This allows NetScaler Gateway to forward LDAP credentials (which are defined as the primary authentication) to the StoreFront server. We also need to set **Clientless Access** to **Allow** and define the **Plug-in Type** to **Java**, as shown in the following screenshot:

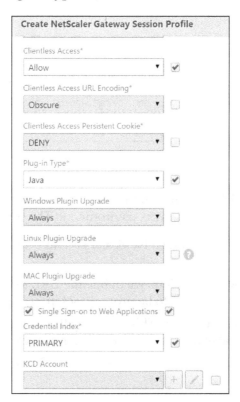

The **Credential Index** and **Plug-in Type** fields are by default set to **PRIMARY** and Windows/Mac plugin respectively at the global level, so we might need to override the global values. In case of multiple vServers, it is better to define these settings at the vServer level instead of the global level. Note also that even though we specified the **Plug-in Type** as **Java**, this is for legacy purposes, and users will be allowed to access using their regular Citrix Receiver.

In the **Security** pane, all we need to do is make sure that the **Default Authorization Action** option is set to **Allow**, as shown in the following screenshot:

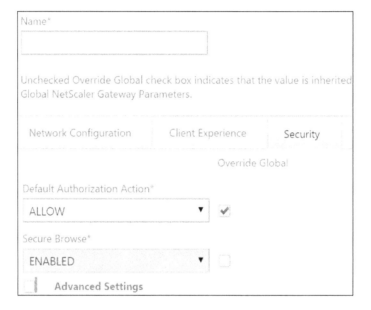

This ensures that the users are actually allowed to log in and access the resources.

Next, we have the **Published Applications** pane. This is where we enter the information needed to access our Citrix environment. The settings are as follows:

- **ICA Proxy**: Here, we define if NetScaler should tunnel ICA traffic through port 443.

- **Web Interface Address**: Here, we define the URL to the StoreFront Citrix web receiver, which needs to be properly set up using HTTPS.

- **Web Interface Portal Mode**: This defines if the web interface should appear with full graphical experience or use the compact view.

- **Single Sign-on Domain**: This defines which AD domain should be used for single sign-on.

- **Citrix Receiver Homepage**: This is used to define the URL for clients connecting to a Citrix receiver that does not support StoreFront.

- **Account Services Address**: This is used for e-mail based account discovery for Citrix Receiver. The URL must be in the form of `https://<StoreFront/ AppControllerURL>/Citrix/Roaming/Accounts`. This requires that the DNS must be properly configured. More information can be found at `http://blogs.citrix.com/2013/04/01/configuring-email-based- account-discovery-for-citrix-receiver/`.

Here, we need to set ICA Proxy to **On** and define the URL to the StoreFront address. We can also define a single sign-on domain. The domain name entered here has to match the one set in StoreFront, so the policy should be as shown in the following screenshot:

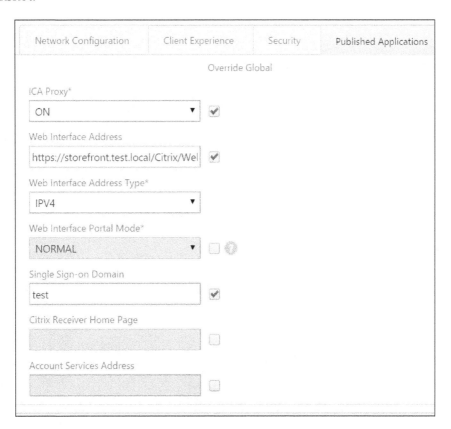

After this is set, we are done with the session policy, and we can click on **Create**. Then we choose the policy and click on **Select** and then **Bind**. This will then associate the policy to the vServer.

Now, the final part that is remaining is to add the STA servers. In the **vServer Creation** window, go to the **Published Applications** option on the right and click on the **+** sign behind STA server to add the servers. It is important to note that the STA servers that are added here need to be the same ones used in Storefront later in the configuration, since the validation of the ICA session is done twice and the STA ID needs to be the same.

 It is recommended that the STA servers be added by IP addresses instead of hostnames. The STA servers that are added here should be identical to those used in StoreFront. If not, we may have issues establishing ICA sessions, and may get some unexplained `1030` or `1110` errors.

We have now fully configured the Gateway function on NetScaler. Now, we have to configure StoreFront to allow remote connections to pass through authentication.

StoreFront integration

Integrating StoreFront requires an existing StoreFront and XenApp/XenDesktop deployment in place. First, we need to add a gateway to StoreFront. This can be done from the GUI by navigating to **StoreFront Administration Console | Gateways**. On the right-hand side here, click on **Add Gateway Server** and then add the information as shown in the following screenshot:

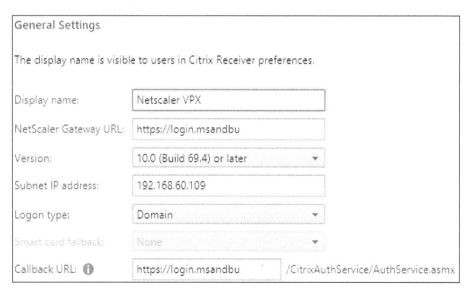

Enter the relevant information. The **Callback URL** field needs to point to the VIP address of NetScaler Gateway. This is needed so that StoreFront can send validation back to the Gateway authentication service. The Subnet IP address is used by StoreFront to identify if a user is connecting from NetScaler. This field is optional for newer releases of NetScaler Gateway. This can also cause an issue if we are using NetScaler to load balance StoreFront, so it is advisable to leave this blank if not necessary.

Now, some issues might occur when communicating back to the callback URL via the external VIP in DMZ. Here, the problem may be twofold. One of the problems you may face here is certificate mismatch. First, open a web browser on the StoreFront server and verify the certificate chain by connecting to the VIP. If it is unsuccessful, add the root or intermediate certificate to the StoreFront server to verify the chain. Also, if DNS is pointing you to the external VIP, you can add an entry to the location in the local hosts file on the StoreFront server, where you enter the FQDN of the VIP server and the internal VIP.

The second problem that might occur is a firewall issue, for example, if StoreFront is located in the intranet zone and is not allowed to communicate back to the VIP, which is located in DMZ. If you are unable to communicate back to the internal VIP because of network restrictions, you can add a dummy VIP to NetScaler, which resides in the internal network with the SNIP. All you need to do to create a new vServer is add STAs and a certificate and alter the StoreFront `hosts` file to point to the dummy VIP instead of the external VIP, which resides in DMZ. This will allow the callback URL to communicate properly.

Now for the final part; we need to go to the **Stores** node, and on the right-hand side of the console, click on the **Enable Remote Access** option of the store we want to enable remote access for. Here, we have to specify how and when resources will be available. The settings are as follows:

- **None**: This option means that only local users on the internal network will be able to access the store.

- **No VPN Tunnel**: This option makes resources available directly to NetScaler Gateway and does not require the use of the NetScaler Gateway plugin.

- **Full VPN Tunnel**: This option makes resources only available through an SSL VPN. This requires a NetScaler Gateway plugin.

As ICA Proxy requires only Citrix Receiver, we choose **No VPN Tunnel**, and we mark the NetScaler appliance that we added earlier.

Next, we need to enable pass-through authentication from the **Authentication** pane in StoreFront. This is needed as users are entering their credentials in NetScaler Gateway, and we want them to sign in automatically to the StoreFront site. The following screenshot shows how to enable pass-through authentication:

One last thing we need to configure in StoreFront is beacons. Beacons are used to identify if a user is coming externally or internally. You can read the Citrix article on how to set up beacons at `https://docs.citrix.com/en-us/storefront/3/integrate-with-netscaler-and-netscaler-gateway/sf-configure-beacon.html`. Now, we have successfully set up and configured ICA Proxy.

 Beacons are only validated for users connecting using Citrix Receiver directly, users that are going via the web receiver will not be probed using beacons and are always treated as external users.

One thing that is important to note is that ICA Proxy allows for client-initiated renegotiation by default after establishing an SSL connection. This applies to every virtual server that uses SSL, and that is created in NetScaler. Because of security vulnerability in the SSL and TLS protocols, an attacker may be allowed to inject a custom packet inside a secure session when it starts. A free tool is available at `https://www.ssllabs.com`, which we can use to find out if our service is vulnerable to such an attack. In the following screenshot, we can see that our solution is vulnerable to a client renegotiation attack:

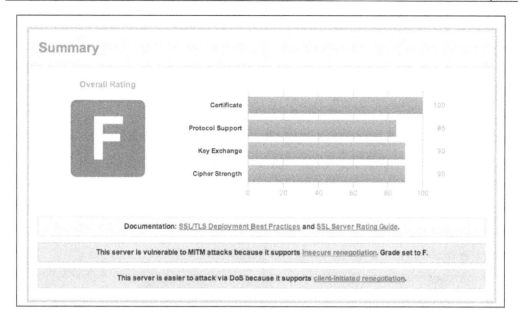

There is a workaround that we can deploy in NetScaler to disable this attack. We can do this by using the following CLI command:

```
Set ssl parameter -denySSLrenegNONSECURE
```

We should also disable SSL3 on the vServer since it has known vulnerabilities such as PODDLE. SSL3 can be disabled by going into the vServer configuration, then going into SSL parameters, and then removing the checkbox before SSLv3, as shown in the following screenshot:

SSL Parameters

☐ Enable DH Param   ☐ SSL Redirect
☐ Enable DH Key Expire Size Limit   ☐ SNI Enable
☑ Enable Ephemeral RSA   ☑ Send Close-Notify

Refresh Count   Clear Text Port

`0`   `0`

☑ Enable Session Reuse   PUSH Encryption Trigger

Time-out

`120`   ⓘ   Always ▼

☐ Enable Cipher Redirect
☐ SSLv2 Redirect
☐ Client Authentication

Protocol

☐ SSLv2   ☐ SSLv3   ☑ TLSv1   ☑ TLSv11   ☑ TLSv12

Deploying VPN

In some cases, users may need to deploy a full VPN solution as it allows a client to become a part of the internal network using the NetScaler Gateway plugin. With the use of the NetScaler Gateway plugin, we also have Endpoint analysis that allows us to scan a client for specific processes, or check if the client has antivirus active and configured. In version 10.5, Citrix added OPSWAT support. OPSWAT is a library that allows us to perform granular scans of an endpoint before it is allowed access.

Configuring the use of regular VPN with NetScaler Gateway is not much different from ICA Proxy. We need the following:

- A NetScaler Gateway vServer with a name, a port, and an IP address
- A vServer set to non ICA-mode
- A trusted certificate
- An authentication policy
- A session policy

The only difference here is that we need to set the vServer to non ICA-mode and we need to change the session policy.

We can also add a pre-authentication policy to allow NetScaler to check client-side security before users are authenticated. This method makes sure that a device is compliant before being allowed to communicate with internal resources.

When we are creating the session profile, there are attributes that should be configured in the **Client Experience** pane. There are multiple settings that define how a VPN tunnel should behave, so it is important to know what each feature does. The settings are as follows:

- **Split Tunnel**: This is used to define if all client traffic or only traffic for destined servers in the network should go through the gateway in a CVPN connection.
- **Client Idle Time-out (mins)**: This defines how long NetScaler waits before it disconnects the session when there is no user activity. This only applies to NetScaler plugins.
- **Plug-in Type**: This defines what kind of plugin is offered to the user, either Windows-/Mac-based or Java-based.

- **Windows, Linux & Mac Plugin Upgrade**: If the vServer should do upgrades of the EPA clients when connecting. Since NetScaler might have updates to the EPA client in case of a firmware upgrade, we can now select if we want the vServer to offer the upgrade. If we have other deployment solutions, we should have this switched off.

- **Single Sign-on to Web Applications**: This allows NetScaler to perform SSO either for the web interface / StoreFront or if we have set a custom homepage to be the SharePoint site.

- **Credential Index**: This defines which authentication credentials are forwarded to the web application. Here, we can choose from the primary or the secondary authentication set.

- **Single Sign-on with Windows**: This allows the Gateway plugin to authenticate to NetScaler using Windows credentials.

There are some exceptions here. If the **Split Tunnel** option is disabled, it means that all endpoint traffic is routed through NetScaler. If it is enabled, it means only traffic that is destined for the internal network is routed through NetScaler. This also means that if the feature is enabled, we need to define which IP address or range of addresses the gateway should intercept. This is done using something called an intranet application, which is available as an option under the vServer pane. Here, we can define a range of IP addresses or a single IP address that the Gateway will intercept for the client. There are some differences here. For example, for Java-based clients, we need to define intranet applications as proxy-based, and for regular Windows/Mac clients, we need to define the intranet applications as transparent. We cannot combine these two types of intranet applications.

Also, should we require giving a connected client a dedicated IP address, we will have to define intranet IPs that will act like a DHCP server. Here, we can define a range of IP addresses that can be given to users. These intranet IPs can be bound to an AAA user, an AAA group, a vServer, or they can be bound at a global level. IP addresses that are bound to a user take priority over the other options.

Now, under the **Published Applications** pane, we need to define the following:

- **ICA Proxy**: This should be set to Off, as the client will have a full VPN connection and does not need the Gateway to proxy traffic

- **Web Interface Address**: This should be defined to allow clients to connect to the StoreFront site

- **Single Sign-on Domain**: This defines which AD domain can be used for single sign-on

When users connect to this vServer now, they will be presented with a download option that allows them to download the NetScaler Gateway plugin, and they will be redirected to the StoreFront site.

As a part of NetScaler Gateway plugin, we have the option to perform scans on the client both as part of the pre-authentication policy process and as part of the security configuration session policy with a client security check, which has the option to place a client in quarantine group if, for instance, antivirus is switched off. The pre-authentication profile has the option to delete files on the computer or cancel processes before it is allowed connection. An example might be a client that is connecting where we have split tunneling switched off. The client connecting has a torrent client running, which consumes a large number of resources and will now start routing this traffic via the NetScaler. Using a pre-authentication policy, we can make the endpoint client scan for this and then shut down the process before the client is allowed to connect.

Up until now, we have only used the ns_true expression when defining policies. Now it is time to explore OPSWAT further, which we discussed briefly earlier. OPSWAT is an open source library that allows us to perform granular scans of expressions based upon, for instance, whether drive encryption is enabled or antivirus is running. OPSWAT can be run using a regular session policy or a pre-auth policy or as part of a security check.

When setting up a session profile under the Expression pane, we have an option called OPSWAT EPA editor. If we click on this button, we are given two options: Mac and Windows. From there, we have multiple options to choose from. For instance, if we choose Antivirus, then choose Generic Antivirus Product Scan, and then click on the + sign, we have the option to check if the device connecting has a specific version, has real-time protection enabled, and so on.

When we have configured a policy, we can also define frequency. If this is set to blank, the scan will only be performed once. Frequency scans only work on SSL VPN–based sessions.

Now, after we are done altering the expression, we can bind it to the vServer as show in the following screenshot:

This will allow users who have antivirus with real-time protection enabled access to the vServer. Clients who do not fulfill the expression requirements are not granted access, and thus they will not trigger the session policy.

Now, even though the VPN uses the NetScaler Gateway plugin to establish a connection, we still need Citrix Receiver to establish a connection to the Citrix environment and process ICA sessions. It is possible to integrate these two clients. If a user has Citrix Receiver installed previously and they then install the NetScaler Gateway plugin, they will get a new option under **Citrix Receiver Applet** | **About** | **Advanced** | **Access Gateway Settings**. From here, users can start a full VPN session directly using Citrix Receiver when they are connected by clicking on **Login** from the **Access Gateway Settings** option.

So after these settings are configured, you will have successfully configured a VPN solution on our Gateway. An important point to note is that in some cases, you may face issues with building a VPN tunnel. This issue occurs with some firewalls. In such a case, you may consider using MAC-based forwarding.

Deploying clientless access

Clientless access is a basic browser-based VPN solution, where users are presented with a homepage when they log in and from there they can access file shares, web applications, and other settings depending on what is defined in the session policy.

In order to allow clientless access, we need to define some settings in the Session Policy section of the **Client Experience** pane. The settings are as follows:

- **URL for Web-Based Email**: This is used for logging into web-based e-mail solutions, such as Exchange OWA. This will appear as a pane within the clientless access session policy window.

- **Session Time-out (mins)**: This defines how long NetScaler waits before it disconnects the session when there is no network traffic.

- **Clientless Access**: This defines if the SSL-based VPN should be enabled or disabled.

- **Clientless Access URL Encoding**: This defines whether the URL of internal web applications are obscured or are in clear text and visible to the users.

- **Clientless Access Persistent Cookie**: This is needed to access certain features in SharePoint, such as opening and editing documents.

- **Client Cleanup Prompt**: This is used to control the display of the client cleanup prompt after exiting an SSL VPN session.

- **Single Sign-on to Web Applications**: This allows NetScaler to do SSO either for the web interface / StoreFront or if we have set a custom homepage to be the SharePoint site.

- **Credential Index**: This defines which authentication credentials are forwarded to the web application. Here, we can choose from the primary or the secondary authentication set.

In the **Published Applications** pane, we define the following settings in the request profile:

- **Web Interface Address**: Here, we define the URL to the StoreFront receiver

- **Web Interface Portal Mode**: This defines whether the web interface should appear with full graphical experience or use the compact view

- **Single Sign-on Domain**: Here, we define which AD domain should be used for single sign-on

Now, in order to activate Clientless Access, we only need to set the vServer to non ICA-only and set Clientless Access to ON under the session policy. However, other settings can affect this feature. For example, if we add a URL for web-based e-mail, users will have an **E-mail** pane after they log in, which is going to be proxied via NetScaler. This allows them to log in to their e-mail. URL encoding determines if the URL should be masked so that the users never see the real URL when they are browsing a web application. Persistent cookie is needed for some cases, such as using SharePoint. Also, adding the web interface address and defining single sign-on allows NetScaler to display the user's applications within the same clientless access session. Clientless access also gives us features such as Clientless File Sharing and so on.

In order to configure Clientless Access to enumerate applications from Storefront, we need to do some additional configuration. First, we need to change some settings under C:\inetpub\wwwroot\Citrix\storename and web.config.

Then, we change all parameters that have the following settings:

```
<add name="X-Frame-Options" value="deny" />
<add name="Content-Security-Policy" value="frame-ancestors 'none'" />
```

Next, we alter the values from deny to allow and from none to self.

The last thing we need to do is add the AD domain that we are accessing, in order to allow Storefront integration to work with Clientless Access. This can be added under **NetScaler Gateway** | **Global Settings** | **Configure Domain** for clientless access followed by entering the domain name there.

Binding the features together

We have three different features that we have gone through, and each of them gives us some functionality, for example, whether we want all the different features to be available to the user at the same time and give the users the option to choose between different features.

> An important point to note is that using all these features on the same vServer requires universal licenses for all the users connecting to it. So, in some cases, it may be more beneficial to create two vServers, where you have one for VPN services and one for ICA Proxy.

If we want to have a single web portal where we want to give the users the ability to choose the kind of resource they need, we need to make a change to the default session policy that they use. Under **Session Policy**, go to the request profile that is bound to it and then click on the **Client Experience** pane. Here, click on the **Advanced** button. In the menu, we have an option called **Client Choices**. By enabling this, the users will get an option to choose what type of feature they need when logging in to the web portal, as shown in the following screenshot:

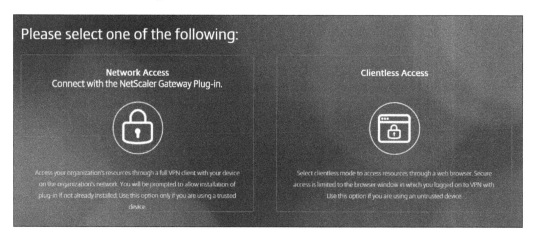

The options presented here are dependent on what is configured in the session policy. For example, if Clientless Access is not defined, it will not show up as an option here. If we have not entered a web interface address and STA is not available, Citrix XenApp will not show up as an option. Lastly, if we have set the vServer to basic mode, it will automatically go to the StoreFront server after authentication. Another option we have is to use expressions. We can use expressions to filter sessions based on user agents, IP addresses, and so on. For example, we want to create a dedicated session policy to be applied only to Android devices and the default session policy to be applied to all other devices that are connecting. For Android devices, the following CLI expression declares that the connecting client must have a user agent string, which contains Citrix Receiver and Android:

```
REQ.HTTP.HEADER User-Agent CONTAINS CitrixReceiver&&REQ.HTTP.HEADER
User-Agent CONTAINS Android/
```

 A list of different expressions that can be used for different client types can be found at http://support.citrix.com/proddocs/topic/access-gateway-10/agee-clg-session-policies-overview-con.html.

Then, we create a custom session policy that is bound to that expression containing the specific configuration for our Android devices. We then use the general ns_true expression to apply to the rest and bind a session policy for the rest of the devices. Also, remember that the Android policy needs to have a lower priority than the other one, as ns_true applies to all clients that are connecting to the vServer.

One last feature that we can use is filtering based upon the AD group. For example, we want users who are part of the executives group to gain access to everything in the corporate network and the regular users to gain access to some of the network. The way this operates is that when a user connects to the web portal, we can use NetScaler to get the list of the AD groups that the user is a member of from Active Directory, and find the first policy that is bound to one of the AD groups. It is important to note that user policies are processed before vServer and global policies. Therefore, if we have two session policies—one bound for the vServer and another for a user group—the user group policy will win.

In order to use this feature, we must first enable the authentication policy to get the list of the AD groups that the user who is connecting is a part of. This can be done by making sure that the **memberOf** attribute is entered in the authentication policy in the **Group Attribute** field. This is shown in the following screenshot:

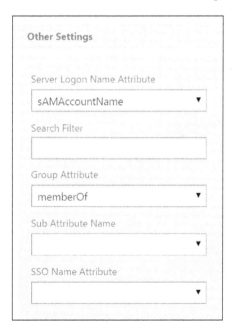

After that is done, we need to go into the Policy Manager to create the AD groups. This can be found in the **NetScaler Gateway** pane. Here, we must first create a group under **AAA Groups**. The group name must be identical to the group name in the AD. Now, we can start by clicking on the **+** sign and then assign policies to the group. The policy should then appear as shown in the following screenshot:

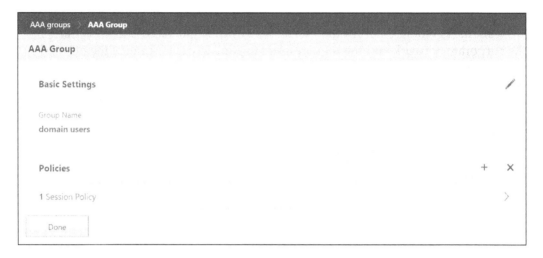

Here we can define different session policies, audit policies, and for instance, intranet IP policies based upon an AD user group, which makes it a lot easier to scope rules to different departments.

Unified Gateway

Unified Gateway is a new feature that was introduced in software version 11. It is a unified portal that allows access to all our users' applications in the same interface using the same URL. This might be XenApp/XenDesktop applications, or it might be SaaS, on-premises web-applications or other services that are load balanced using NetScaler. This means that we can set up multiple services for a customer using the same URL. This feature is built-up of other features in NetScaler, which has been around for many years, but Citrix did a bit of a polishing job of the Clientless Access portal.

In order to set up a Unified Gateway, we have to run the wizard available in the management portal. The wizard is configured to allow deployment of traditional NetScaler Gateway as well. Click on the **Unified Gateway** feature and choose **Get Started**. From there choose **Single Public Access Point**. Now, there are five feature that we need to configure in this deployment to get it up and running:

- Virtual Server Configuration
- Server Certificate
- Authentication
- Portal Theme
- Applications

It is important to remember here that the virtual server is going to be represented as a content switching virtual server and not a NetScaler Gateway vServer. The reason for this is that a content switching server has the ability to redirect to backend resources based upon URL or hostnames, for instance. The wizard will also deploy a NetScaler Gateway vServer, but the IP address is set to 0.0.0.0 and will be referenced from the content switching vServer for Citrix sessions.

So, let's start by entering a name and an IP-address for the Unified Gateway. Next, add a server certificate to the Gateway, similar to what you did earlier when setting up ICA Proxy. Note, however, that the certificate step here will validate the certificate chain, so if it is missing RootCA or intermediate CA, you will get an error message like this, and you will need to upload the missing CA certificate as well.

Next, add an authentication policy. This policy will apply to all users who try to access the gateway.

Now you need to define a portal theme. This defines how the GUI of the portal should look. By default, there are two different themes you can choose from, **Default** and **GreenBubble**. The last one is the one used on StoreFront as well, but you can create a custom one if you want to, using the web management, which is covered later in this chapter.

Finally, define different applications that are going to be accessible from within the portal.

We have five different application profiles that we can bind to a unified gateway. First, it is split into two different categories: either it's a Citrix XenApp/XenDesktop environment or it's a web-based application. Within the second category, we have four different types of applications that can be added:

- Intranet Applications
- Clientless Access
- SaaS applications
- Preconfigured applications on NetScaler

Intranet applications are web-based applications that need to be available for VPN users. When adding an intranet application, NetScaler automatically creates content switching rules based upon the URL to redirect VPN users to the correct vServer. Intranet applications can either be accessed using Clientless Access or with a full VPN client. When adding an application, we have the option to **Make this application accessible through the unified gateway URL** as shown in the screenshot. If this is turned off, users will require full VPN access, and we can have security policies such as preauthentication scans before the client is allowed access.

Clientless Access applications are typically applications such as Exchange and SharePoint and allow for SSO and integrated access from within the Unified Gateway portal.

SaaS applications are public applications hosted in most cases in a public cloud provider; this can be services such as Sharefile, Office365, Dropbox, and so on. We can also allow NetScaler to act as an SAML SP and to authenticate on behalf of the users. This of course requires federated setup like with Active Directory Federation Services.

Preconfigured applications are applications that are pre-hosted by NetScaler and are running and are accessible using a vServer. So we have to point the application to an existing vServer and enter an absolute URL.

Now all these different resources are then added as a bookmark, which can be displayed under **NetScaler Gateway | Resources | Bookmarks**:

As we can see in the preceding screenshot, NetScaler is used as a reverse proxy for some applications, and some require full VPN access to be able to work. Now, running the Unified Gateway wizard will actually publish all applications to all users. In order to publish applications to specific users or groups, we need to use the NetScaler Gateway Policy Manager. Choose either user or groups and then add bookmarks to those objects.

As mentioned, we can also add a XenApp/XenDesktop environment to the unified gateway. In that case, we need to add the StoreFront Server FQDN, Site Path for web receiver, Single-sign on domain, Store name, STA servers, IP address of the storefront server, and protocol and port number. After that is done, the Unified Gateway will enumerate all applications that a particular user has access to when logging in.

Now using all these different options, we have a gateway that allows users to access all their different applications. These could be SaaS, on-premise, or Windows-based applications.

Tuning

Now that we have gone through some of the different deployment types available in NetScaler Gateway, we should also take a closer look at fine-tuning the deployment setup with some simple changes.

Redirection

First, let us take a closer look at redirection, as by default NetScaler Gateway answers only on port 443, which uses HTTPS. Many users forget to type https when accessing the portal, and therefore are not able to locate it. The NetScaler Gateway wizard has the option to set up redirection from http to https automatically.

By default, a vServer consists of an IP address and a port. The Gateway vServer responds to port 443. So in order to perform a redirect, we need to set up a vServer using port 80, as it has the option to redirect. This can be done with the help of the following steps:

1. Go to **Traffic Management** | **Load Balancing** | **Virtual Servers** and click on **Add**.

2. Enter the same IP address as the regular Gateway vServer, and choose the regular HTTP in the **Port** field. Then click on **OK**.

3. Then click on **Continue** to get the advanced features. Next, go to the **Protection** pane on the right-hand side. There, you have an option called **Redirect URL** where you enter the FQDN of the vServer with HTTPS in the front.

When this is done, click on **OK**. It should appear as in the following screenshot:

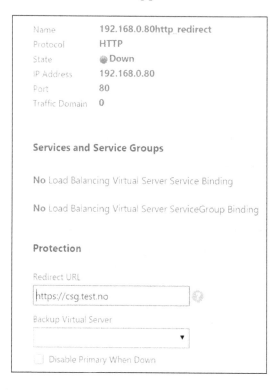

 Make sure that the redirect URL has the full prefix as `https://url.com/` with the forward slash at the end, or else some security scanners might see it as an XSS vulnerability.

Profiles

NetScaler can optimize connections using different TCP parameters, HTTP parameters, and net profiles. Many of the optimization parameters are set in different types of TCP profiles, and these can be viewed under **System | Profiles | TCP Profiles**.

Different profiles are useful in different scenarios and have different advantages depending on the network they are used in and the endpoints that are connecting. By default, all vServers that are created in NetScaler use `nstcp_default_profile`. This profile makes sure that it works properly in all networks.

Let us take a look at some of the different profiles:

- `nstcp_default_tcp_lfp`: This profile is best suited for high-bandwidth WAN and low packet loss environments. This profile, however, does not use Window scaling or selective ACK. It uses the default TCP congestion algorithm, TCP reno.

- `nstcp_default_tcp_lnp`: This profile is best suited for low-bandwidth WAN and high packet loss environments.

- `nstcp_default_tcp_lan`: This profile is best suited for internal networks that are connected using LAN.

- `nstcp_internal_apps`: This profile should only be used for internal services on NetScaler and should not be used on any other network services.

- `nstcp_default_XA_XD_profile`: This profile is best suited for ICA Proxy solutions and ICA traffic. This is because it uses SACK, Nagle, and Window scaling which allows for much better TCP performance for ICA traffic since it consists of small packets.

Now, for a NetScaler Gateway vServer using ICA Proxy, it is highly recommended to use `nstcp_default_xa_xd_profile`. You can add this setting in NetScaler Gateway through the vServer by going into the **Advanced** pane and clicking on **TCP Profiles**. When using a TCP profile, which is not the general one, you should test it properly before implementing it. Note, however, TCP tuning will be covered in a later chapter.

Another option where we can use profiles is if we are in a situation where we have different internal zones and different VIPs for our end users, and we need to make sure that a particular VIP uses a particular SNIP address. There is no direct relation between a VIP and an SNIP. If a NetScaler Gateway server were to connect to a StoreFront server, it would use the SNIP closest to it. If we have multiple internal zones, this would not work properly. This is where network profiles come in.

The network profile feature allows us to define the use of a specific source IP address or multiple addresses. In order to use network profiles, we must first create a network profile that contains the source IP address we wish NetScaler to use when initiating a connection to the backend servers. This can be done under **System | Network | Net Profiles** by clicking on **Add**. Now we can enter a name for the profile, choose an IP address or multiple addresses (IP set), and then click on **Create**.

After we have created a network profile, we have to attach it to the different features that use an SNIP for backend connectivity. They are as follows:

- Virtual Server
- Service
- Service Groups
- Monitor

So, if we need to bind a specific network profile to a NetScaler Gateway vServer, we need to go to **vServer | Advanced | Net Profile** and choose the network profile that we created earlier.

GUI customization

With NetScaler 11, we now have the option to customize the portal GUI from within the management portal. In previous builds, this was not an option, and we had to execute some custom shell commands to create a template theme and then adjust the CSS files and HTML files ourselves.

In order to create a custom theme, we need to go into **NetScaler Gateway | Portal themes** and then click on **Add**. From here, we choose the kind of template theme we want, give it a name, and click OK.

Following this, we can change the common attributes such as locale, font size, font color, background image, logos, and so on. When we click on **OK**, we are given more options as follows:

- Login page title, password, and field name
- EPA Page
- EPA Error Page
- Post EPA Page
- VPN Connection Page
- Portal Home Page

It also allows us to hide certain sections such as File Shares and so on from the GUI. More advanced customization requires access using the SSH client or using FTP. This allows us to create custom HTML pages and alter every CSS setting, as described in this blog post at `https://msandbu.wordpress.com/2013/11/04/netscaler-tips-and-tricks/`.

Testing

Now, the setup and configuration of NetScaler Gateway with different options is complete. Before putting it into production, make sure that you have tested it properly. A quick checklist that you should go through is as follows:

- Different clients
- Different features such as Clientless Access, VPN, and ICA Proxy
- Trusted certificates on different devices
- Authentication from different devices
- Use of the latest version of Citrix Receiver
- Examination of the network traffic flow in case something is not working properly

Summary

In this chapter, we went through many of the different deployment types of the NetScaler Gateway function. We went through ICA Proxy, VPN using the NetScaler Gateway plugin, SSL-based VPN, and the different scenarios based on these.

Many deployments require the use of NetScaler Gateway, not just in XenDesktop but also in the newly released version of XenMobile. We cannot cover all the different deployment types, so I recommend heading over to eDocs on Citrix for more information about the different deployment types. This eDoc is located at `https://docs.citrix.com/en-us/netscaler-gateway/11.html`.

In the next chapter, we will explore load balancing and how we can use it for different technologies, such as the roles feature in Citrix and for other products, such as Exchange, SharePoint, and other generic web services.

3
Load Balancing

Load-balanced services are accessed by users every day, such as when they book a plane ticket on a website, watch the news, or access social media. By using load balancing, we have the ability to distribute user requests or client requests for content and applications across multiple backend servers where the content is located. In this chapter, we will cover the following topics:

- How load balancing works
- How to load balance a generic web application
- How to load balance Citrix services such as the XML service and DDC servers
- How to load balance Microsoft products such as SharePoint, Exchange, and MSSQL

A load-balanced service within NetScaler allows us to distribute user requests from different sources based upon different parameters and algorithms, such as least bandwidth or least connections. It also provides persistency, which allows us to maintain a session on the same server. These features allow us to redirect clients to a backend server, for example, a server with the least connections used.

A regular generic load-balanced service might look a bit like the one shown in the following figure. We have two backend web servers that answer on port 80, and they are publicly accessible via a VIP address, which is the load-balanced service. So, in essence, a load-balanced service in NetScaler consists of the following:

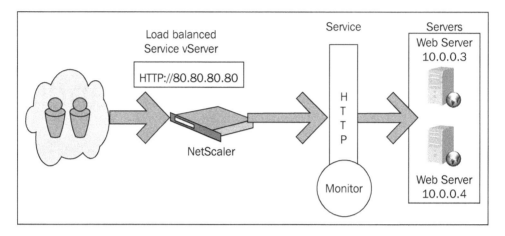

- **Servers**: These are the backend servers that host a service.
    - The IP address and server name are **10.0.0.3** and server1 respectively, and we have **10.0.0.4**, which is server2.

- **Service**: Here, we define which service is hosted on the backend servers. We also define a monitor, which is used to check if the service is responding on the backend server.
    - The service name is IIS1
    - The IP address and server name are 10.0.0.3 and server1 respectively
    - The protocol and port are HTTP and 80 respectively
    - By defining a monitor, HTTP allows the service object to check if the server is responding to HTTP traffic
    - We also perform the same procedure for server2

- **Virtual server**: Here, we define the IP, port, and protocol on which the load-balanced service will answer; the kind of service is attached at the backend; and how it will load balance between the different services at the back.

- **vServer name**: The vServer name is IIS. This field is only for description.

- **VIP address**: This is the external address of the load-balanced service. In this example, we are using `80.80.80.80`.

- **Protocol and Port**: This is the protocol and port on which this service should respond. Here, it is `HTTP` and `80` respectively.

- **Services or Service Groups**: This defines which backend services are going to be included in the load-balanced object. Here, they are IIS1 and IIS2.

- **Load-balancing method**: This defines what kind of load balancing method is chosen.

If we have multiple backend servers hosting the same service, it is much more convenient to use service groups. This allows us to easily bind a service against multiple servers simultaneously.

When starting the deployment of load-balanced services, we need to have the basic configuration in place, such as placement of SNIP to allow communication with backend servers. A quick rule of thumb is:

- Initial setup with NSIP
- Platform license in place
- SNIP defined for backend connectivity
- Backend servers added to server list
- Services bound to the backend server
- Monitor bound to a service/service group

To begin, we need to enable the load balancing feature. This can be done either by right-clicking on the load balancing menu under **Traffic Management** in the GUI and clicking on **Enable**, or by using the following CLI command:

```
Enable ns feature lb
```

Load balancing a generic web application

In order to deploy a load-balanced web application, we first need to have servers in place that respond to some sort of a network service. In this example, we have two **Internet Information Servers (IIS)** running on Windows Server. These are accessible via the IPs `10.0.0.2` and `10.0.0.3` internally, and they respond to traffic HTTP on port `80`.

First, we add the IP addresses to the server list. This can be done by going to **Traffic Management | Load Balancing | Servers**, and clicking on **Add**. Here, we just enter the IP address of the backend servers and click on **Create**. This must be done for every backend server. Next, we add a service to the servers by going to **Traffic Management | Load Balancing | Services**, and clicking on **Add**. Here, we have many different options. First, we need to choose the server we entered earlier under **Existing Server**, choose a type of protocol, enter a port number, and give the service a name and click on **OK**.

Now, we can add a new monitor to the service by clicking on the **Service to Load balancing Monitor Binding** under **Monitors**. By default, a service will have a monitor bound to it, but this is a TCP-default, which will basically check the port using a TCP handshake on the backend server and may not give us information about whether the server is working as expected. Depending on the service we are load balancing, we may need to change monitors to something else—there may be some specific port or protocol that we need to use.

 Monitors are what make load balancing unique. Unlike regular round-robin solutions, they probe the backend servers and provide NetScaler with backend server health status.

We have other types of monitors that we can use as well. All the default monitors are listed under **Traffic Management | Load Balancing | Monitors**. There are many types of built-in monitors that we can use, some of which are explained as follows:

- **TCP**: This monitor checks the availability using the TCP three-way handshake
- **HTTP**: This monitor uses HTTP's GET request
- **PING**: This monitor uses ICMP
- **TCPS**: This monitor checks the availability using the TCP three-way handshake and a successful SSL handshake
- **HTTPS**: This monitor uses HTTP's GET request and a successful SSL handshake

All the monitors have parameters that define how often they should probe a service before they set it as offline. Some monitors also have extended parameters. This can be viewed by opening a monitor, clicking on **Edit**, and going into the **Special Parameters** pane.

These monitors listed here are just some examples. We also have monitors that have the suffix ecv. These are used when we need to send a specific payload with a monitor. For example, if we want to check for custom headers on a web server, we can use the **http-ecv** monitor. The same can be done with other monitors as well.

Some monitors are not built-in by default. We can add custom monitors for the Citrix Web Interface, XML service, DDC, and so on. These can be added by going to **Monitors | Add**. Then under **Types**, there are different Citrix services that we can add a custom monitor to. For example, if we choose **CITRIX-XML-SERVICE**, we need to specify an application name in the **Special Parameters** pane. If we click on **Create**, we can use this monitor when setting up a load-balanced XML service.

Now that we have created a service in NetScaler for each backend server that is hosting the service, we are almost ready for load balancing. It is also important to note that a service is bound to a port. This means we cannot create a service on a server that is bound to a service.

If we want to limit the amount of bandwidth or number of clients that can access the backend service, we can add thresholds to the service. This can be done by going to **Service | Thresholds**. This is useful if you have some backend servers that have limited bandwidth, or when you wish to guard yourself against a DDoS attack.

Note that we can also specify our own TCP profiles and net profiles for the backend connections here as well. For instance, if we want to specify that traffic going to a specific service should use a specific SNIP, we can use a custom net profile to do that. Also, for resources stored in the datacenter, we typically have high-end connections and can use more TCP features and a higher MTU rate, so we can use a custom TCP profile here as well. This will increase the efficiency of backend connections.

After we have created a service for each of our servers, we can go on to create the load-balanced virtual server. Go back to **Traffic Management | Load Balancing | Virtual Servers**, and click on **Add**. There are multiple settings that we need to set here. First, we need to enter a name, IP address, port, and protocol. Now, the kind of protocol that we choose here is essential. For example, if we choose SSL, and the backend servers are responding on regular HTTP traffic, NetScaler will automatically perform SSL offloading. This means that NetScaler will terminate the SSL connection at the VIP and then fulfill regular HTTP requests to the backend servers. The advantage of this is that the backend web servers do not need to use CPU cycles to handle SSL traffic.

When we enable SSL as a protocol on the vServer, the **Certificates** pane will be enabled, and here, we need to add an SSL certificate for our service. It is important that DNS is configured properly. If the DNS name and the subject name in the certificate do not match, we will get a warning, as NetScaler will not be able to validate the certificate. Also, it is important that we have the full SSL chain in place. If not, NetScaler cannot validate the certificate.

If company requirements are that all traffic needs to be encrypted from client to server, we can use SSL bridging. This enables NetScaler to bridge traffic from the clients to the backend servers. When we enable SSL bridging, NetScaler disables some features, as it cannot see into the packets because the traffic is encrypted. For example, features such as content switching, SureConnect, or cache redirection will not work. Also, with SSL bridging, we do not need to add a certificate, as it is already available in the backend servers. So for this example, we will use SSL and add a certificate in the **Certificates** pane. After we have done this, we will bind the backend services or service groups to the vServer. If we do not add a service to the vServer, it will be listed as **DOWN** until a service has been added and assigned. So after we have entered the virtual server information, we can click on **Continue**. This will give us the option to add a service or a service group to the vServer. It is important to note that even if NetScaler is not doing any SSL offloading, we can still benefit from the SSL multiplexing feature that allows more efficient SSL traffic.

After we have added the required information, a certificate, and a service, the vServer should look something like the following screenshot:

Load Balancing Virtual Server

Basic Settings

Name	HTTPS-vServer2
Protocol	SSL
State	Down
IP Address	192.168.0.9
Port	443
Traffic Domain	0

Services and Service Groups

2 Load Balancing Virtual Server Service Bindings

No Load Balancing Virtual Server ServiceGroup Binding

Certificates

1 Server Certificate

1 CA Certificate

Now, we should define the load-balancing methods and persistency. There are multiple ways to load balance between the different services. They are explained as follows:

- **Least connection**: In this method, the backend service with the fewest active connections is used. This is the default method.

- **Round robin**: In this method, the first session is handed to the service that is on top of the list, and the next connection goes to the second service on the list. This continues down the list and then starts over again.

- **Least response time**: In this method, the service that has the fastest response time is used.

- **URL hash**: In this method, when a connection is made to a URL for the first time, NetScaler creates a hash to that URL and caches it. So frequent connections to the same URL will go to the same service.

- **Domain hash**: In this method, when a connection is made to a domain name for the first time, NetScaler creates a hash for that name and caches it. So, frequent connections to the same domain will go to the same service. The domain name is fetched either from the URL or from the HTTP headers.

- **Destination IP hash**: In this method, when a connection is made to a specific IP address for the first time, NetScaler creates a hash for that destination IP and redirects all connections to that IP address through the same service.

- **Source IP hash**: In this method, when a connection is made from an IP address for the first time, for example `10.0.0.1`, NetScaler creates a hash out of the source IP. Frequent connections made from the IP and/or subnet will go to the same service.

- **Source destination IP hash**: In this method, NetScaler creates a hash based upon the source and destination IP. This ensures that a client is connected to the same server.

- **Call ID hash**: In this method, NetScaler creates a hash based upon the Call ID in the SIP header. This makes sure that an SIP session is directed to the same server.

- **Source IP source port hash**: In this method, NetScaler creates a hash based upon the source and source port. This ensures that a particular connection will go to the same server.

- **Least bandwidth**: This method is based upon the service with the least amount of bandwidth usage.

- **Least packets**: This method is based upon the service with the fewest packets.

- **Custom load**: This method allows us to set custom weights.

- **Token**: In this method, NetScaler selects a service based upon a value from the client request using expressions.
- **LRTM**: In this method, NetScaler selects a service based upon the one with the least response time.

Some of the load-balancing methods are explicitly used for some special services and protocols to make sure that when we set up load balancing and want to use a custom load-balancing method, the method is supported by the service. For example, Lync 2013 uses a special NetScaler monitor, which is listed in the setup guide.

Here, we will use the round-robin method. After we have chosen a way to load balance, we can choose how the connection will persist to the service. Again, there are different methods for a connection to persist. They are listed as follows:

- **Source IP**: In this method, connections from the same source IP are persisted to the same server.
- **Cookie insert**: In this method, each client is given a cookie that contains the IP address and the port of the service that the client is accessing. The client uses the cookie to maintain a persistent connection to the same service.
- **SSL session**: This method bases persistency upon the SSL session ID of the client.
- **Rule**: This method is based upon custom-made rules.
- **URL passive**: This method bases persistency upon URL queries.
- **Custom server ID**: In this method, servers can be given a custom server ID, which can be used in URL queries.
- **Destination IP**: In this method, connections to the same destination IP are persisted to the same server.
- **Source and destination IPs**: In this method, connections from the same source IP to the same destination IP are persistent.
- **RTSP session ID**: This method bases persistency upon the RTSP session ID.
- **SIP call ID**: In this method, persistency is based upon the same SIP call ID.

Some of the persistency types are specific to a particular type of vServer, and all persistency types have a timer attached to them. This timer defines how long a connection should persist to a service. You can view more on the different persistency types and the kind of protocol they can be used for at https://docs.citrix.com/en-us/netscaler/11/traffic-management/load-balancing/load-balancing-persistence/persistence.html.

It is very important that we define persistency. For instance, if we are hosting an e-commerce site and users are adding a shopping list, and they are glued to a specific web server, they can continue doing so until they are done. If we have not defined persistency, users find themselves moving from server to server and losing their information about a shopping list, for instance, because the data is stored on a particular server.

> We also have the option to set a backup persistence. This is used when a connection does not support the primary type.

Now, let us explore a bit the more advanced configurations that we can configure on a vServer.

Assigning weights to a service

Assigning weights to a service allows us to distribute load evenly based upon parameters such as hardware. If we have many backend web servers that have 4 GB RAM, and we have newly set up vServers that have 8 GB RAM, then the new ones should have a higher weight. This can be done when we attach a service to a load-balanced vServer. The higher weight we set on a service, the more user-defined traffic/connections it can handle. This is shown in the following screenshot:

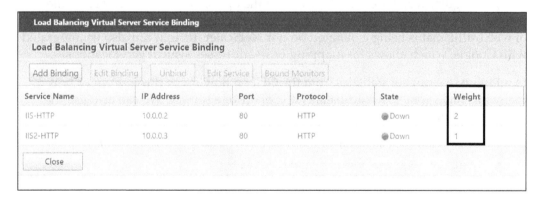

However, it is important to remember that not all load-balancing methods support weighing. For example, all the hashing load-balancing methods and the token load-balancing method do not support weighing.

Redirect URL

Redirect URL is a function that allows us to send a client to a custom web page if the vServer is down. This only works if the vServer is set up using the HTTP or HTTPS protocols. This can be useful for instances where we have a planned maintenance or some unplanned failures, and we want to redirect users to a specific web page, where we have posted information about what is happening. This feature can be configured under **vServer | Protection | Redirect URL**.

Logging and statistics

In many cases, when load balancing web servers, you will want to have logging in place, which you can use to get detailed statistics of sessions that have gone against the web servers. By default, when setting up NetScaler, all traffic initiated will come from a Citrix SNIP address, which makes the log file useless as they all contain the same IP. One option that we can have is to use the Insert Client IP Address option. This will make NetScaler insert the client-ip, from where the original request comes within the HTTP header. By default, when this feature is enabled, the HTTP header will have the mark client-ip. This setting is enabled for each service and can be configured under **Traffic Management | Load Balancing | Services | Settings |** Insert Client IP address.

Also, for regular web-based traffic, we have the option to deploy Citrix NetScaler Insight. This allows for Appflow logging and provides detailed insights on the kind of web traffic that is being generated on our NetScaler. Insight can also be integrated with Google, which allows for mapping of IP addresses against geo-locations.

In addition, we can get statistics from the GUI on how much throughput or how many hits have gone to a load-balanced vServer or a service. We can also use the following commands from CLI to get a good overview:

- `Stat service servicename detail`
- `Stat lb vServer vservername detail`

Backup vServer and failover

Backup vServer allows us to failover to another vServer, in case the main vServer should go down. This can be configured under **vServer | Protection | Backup vServer**.

 An important point to note is that a NetScaler Gateway vServer can also be configured to be used as a backup vServer.

In addition to handling failover, we can also use the backup vServer to handle excessive traffic in case the primary vServer is flooded. This is known as a spillover. We can define spillover based upon different criteria, such as bandwidth connections. We can then define what the vServer should do if there are too many connections to it, for example, if it should drop new connections, accept them, or redirect them to the backup vServer. These settings can also be configured in the same pane as the failover settings. Here, we need to configure the method and what kind of action we want it to take.

 If we have configured a backup vServer and a redirect URL for the same vServer, then the backup vServer takes precedence over the redirect URL.

We have now gone through the basics of setting up a load-balanced service and some of the advanced configuration that we can set. It is important to remember that Citrix has a long list of different products where they have their own deployment guides.

The deployment guides related to Microsoft products can be found at http://www. citrixandmicrosoft.com/Solutions/Networking.aspx. These guides should always be referenced as they contain best practices and step-by-step details on how you should configure, for instance, NetScaler for Lync.

Now, let's continue with this and use the basics to set up load-balanced services for Citrix XenApp and XenDesktop. Now, there are only certain particular services that we can set up as load balanced in a Citrix environment. They are listed as follows:

- StoreFront/Web Interface
- Desktop delivery controllers
- XML service
- Desktop director
- XenMobile
- ShareFile StorageZone controllers
- TFTP for provisioning servers

 NetScaler includes a set of finished wizards that allow us to easily create a load-balanced service for Citrix services, such as WI, DDC, and XML. Most of the examples in the book do not use the wizard — this is just to give you a better understanding of what happens underneath.

Load balancing StoreFront

StoreFront is the replacement for Web Interface and is included by default in XenDesktop 7. This deployment should be in place before you setting up a load-balanced service for StoreFront. StoreFront should be configured as part of a server group. More information about this can be found in the eDoc located at `https://docs.citrix.com/en-us/storefront/3/sf-configure-server-group.html`.

Before we start configuring a load-balanced service for StoreFront, we need a monitor in place to verify that the StoreFront store is functioning and not just checking if it is responding on HTTP or HTTPS. NetScaler has a built-in monitor that we can use for this purpose, but we have to specify some additional parameters and create it first.

Go to **Load Balancing | Monitors**, and click on **Add**. On the right-hand side of the window, choose **STOREFRONT** from the list, and then go to the **Special Parameters** pane. Enter the name in the **Store Name** field, as shown in the following screenshot:

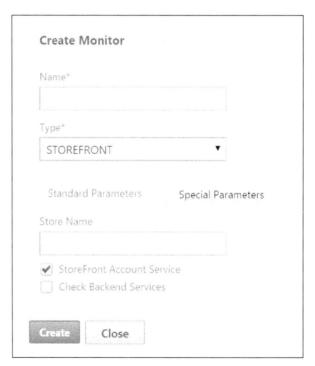

This can be found in the StoreFront administration console.

We also have the option to monitor backend windows services running on the StoreFront server by marking the **Check Backend Services** button.

After this is done, give the monitor a name, and click on **Create**. Now, continue on with the setup as follows:

1. First, add the backend servers that are running StoreFront to the server list.

2. Next, bind a service to the servers. The difference from when we configured the generic web application is that we need to choose the custom-made monitor we created. This will make sure that the StoreFront service is functioning before a client connects to it. Another option we could configure here is allowing NetScaler to insert the client IP into the HTTP header. Because of the way NetScaler operates, the StoreFront server will never actually see the client IP, which is sometimes needed for troubleshooting and logging purposes. We can configure this while setting up the services by going to **Settings | Enable Client IP**. Under the **Header** box, we enter, for example X-Forwarded-For, to distinguish the name in the web server logs. After creating the service for each of the StoreFront servers, it is time to create the vServer.

3. Go to **Virtual Servers** and click on **Add**. Enter an IP address, a port, and a protocol. Lastly, bind the backend services to the vServer. Now, depending on how we want the users to access the StoreFront resource, we need to consider what kind of protocol we set here. For example, if all users are accessing Citrix using the Gateway function, we could choose the **HTTP** protocol and change the URL in the session policy to point to the new VIP created by the load-balanced server. It is, however, best practice to deploy Storefront using SSL, and it should therefore be deployed as such, since most Receiver clients require that Storefront operates on SSL.

4. Next, add a persistency to the vServer, which will allow us to stay connected to the same StoreFront server. The recommended setting here is to use **SOURCE_IP**, and the timeout value should be set to **0**, which means no expiry. This will allow users to reconnect to the same StoreFront server as long as it is responding to requests.

Load balancing a web interface

Setting up a load-balanced web interface is not very different from setting up StoreFront. The main difference is the monitor that is used for the services. NetScaler also has a predefined web interface monitor called **CITRIX-WEB-INTERFACE**, but we have to create it before we can use it. We also have to enter a site path in the **Special Parameters** pane of the monitor window. This monitor checks for resource availability by authenticating an Active Directory user.

You can read more about setting up Web Interface monitoring at `http://support.citrix.com/proddocs/topic/netscaler-load-balancing-93/ns-lb-monitors-builtin-wi-tsk.html`. Other than that, the configuration is the same as it is with StoreFront. Enter the servers, bind the services, and create the load-balanced server.

Load balancing XML Broker

The XML Broker service is needed for communication between the Web Interface/StoreFront and the data collector. Web Interface communicates using XML Broker to get information, such as application availability for a user and available resources.

The XML Broker service is needed in a XenApp/XenDesktop environment and can be deployed as a load-balanced service. Again, Citrix has made a custom monitor available, which we can use to monitor whether the XML Broker service is responding or not.

To add the custom monitor, go to **Load Balancing** | **Monitors**, and click on **ADD**. Here, choose **CITRIX-XML-SERVICE**, and in the **Special Parameters** pane, enter an application name. The default application is Notepad. This monitor will open a connection to the service, and probe the XML Broker service to which it is bound. If the server responds as expected within the configured time period, the monitor marks the service as up. After this is added, we can start adding servers that have the XML service running under servers. Then, we add the XML service under services by choosing **HTML** as the protocol and adding the port on which the XML service is running. Next, we create the load-balanced vServer by choosing protocol **HTTP** and port **80**, and binding the services to the vServer.

> Even though we can choose to create the XML service with HTTP, it is always considered a best practice to use SSL so as to secure communication whenever possible, even if the traffic is internal. Also, if you intend to use HTTP for XML, a best practice is to use another port instead of port 80 so that it does not cause issues for IIS.

When we are finished with the configuration of the vServer, we can now use this IP when connecting to StoreFront or Web Interface. For example, if we want to use the vServer with Storefront, we can add the load-balanced server under **Add Delivery Controllers** | **XenApp** | **Servers**. Here, we can enter the IP address of the load-balanced XML service.

Load balancing the Desktop Delivery Controller

With the release of XenDesktop 7 and the combining of XenApp/XenDesktop architecture, the Desktop Delivery Controller has become a more crucial part to load balance. Yet again, there is a custom monitor that needs to be created called **CITRIX-XD-DDC**. In the **Special Parameters** pane, enter an AD user, which can be used to validate credentials. This is shown in the following screenshot:

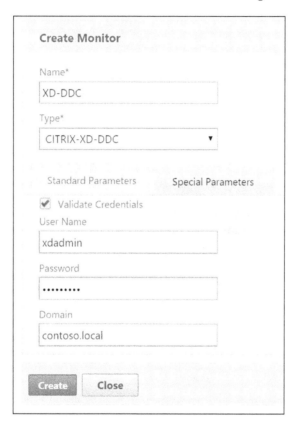

Now, add the servers, bind them to the service, and then create a load-balanced vServer, as we have done for other load-balanced services.

Load balancing TFTP for provisioning servers

This is a new feature that came with NetScaler 10.1. It is the ability to load balance TFTP servers. Before the 10.1 release of NetScaler, this required a great deal of work including the use of **Direct Server Return** (**DSR**) and other options. However, they are no longer required.

An important point to remember is that when you boot a virtual machine using PVS, it uses either PXE or the DHCP options, including options 66 and 67. This guide uses DHCP options to distribute the link to the bootstrap file.

Now, in order to set up load balancing for TFTP properly, we need a monitor that we can use to verify if load balancing is operational. To get a monitor for TFTP, follow the guidelines located at https://www.citrix.com/blogs/2011/01/06/monitoring-tftp-with-citrix-NetScaler-revisited-pvs-edition/.

After creating the monitor, add the servers where the TFTP service resides. Next, create a service for each TFTP server. Here, choose **TFTP** as the protocol, and in the **Port** field, enter 69. Then, bind the custom-made monitor to the service. After this is done, create the load-balanced vServer by entering an IP address, the name, the protocol (TFTP), and the port (69). When this is complete and the vServer has been created, alter the DHCP option 66 to point to the new VIP address that was created in NetScaler.

As a side note, it is also possible to deliver the bootstrap using HTTP instead of TFTP. This scenario is only viable for XenServer, as it uses gPXE, which allows for extra features such as HTTP. This makes it a lot easier to load balance, as we only need to load balance a simple HTTP server and change the option 67 boot filename to point to http://serverip/ARDBP32.BIN. However, this is not supported by Citrix and should only be used in environments where HTTP is a better suited protocol. As always, remember to save the configuration using the GUI or the save config command in CLI.

Make sure you are running build 120 of NetScaler or higher before setting up TFTP load balancing. If you have build 118 or 119, make sure that you do not create a load-balanced TFTP server before setting up high-availability, or else NetScaler will crash. This is a known issue that has been fixed in build 120. You can read more about it at https://www.citrix.com/content/dam/citrix/en_us/documents/downloads/netscaler-adc/NS_10_5_57_7.html.

Load balancing SharePoint 2013

SharePoint has become quite a complex product in its latest releases, from starting out as a portal solution to becoming a complete collaboration platform for businesses. SharePoint can be seen as a web application, and it primarily uses HTTP and HTTPS protocols to deliver content to users. In SharePoint 2013, there have also been some changes in how it operates. For example, Microsoft has introduced a new distributed cache system, which allows a frontend web server to store a login token in memory. This token is also available for other frontend web servers in the farm. This means that we do not need to set up persistency, as all of the authentication tokens are stored in the cache of the web servers. Also, SharePoint 2013 supports SSL offloading, which means that we can use NetScaler to handle SSL traffic and thereby reduce the load on the SharePoint servers by allowing them to respond only on HTTP.

Lastly, as SharePoint has an idea of what is seen as an internal and a public URL (known as alternate access mappings), we need to configure this as well when we set up load balancing, so that SharePoint knows that we have set up a new public URL for the site. We start by adding the frontend SharePoint web servers to the server list by going to **Traffic Management** | **Load Balancing** | **Servers**. Next, we create a service or service group, where we add the servers and bind them to port 80 and protocol HTTP. Then, we add an HTTP monitor to the services and click on **Create**.

 There is also a way to create a custom monitor that actually monitors if a user can authenticate on the SharePoint site. You can read more about this at http://support.citrix.com/article/CTX126201. Take note, however, that this article requires a free Citrix account to log in and read.

Now, we need to create a load-balanced service. Here, we bind the services we created earlier and assign a name, IP address, protocol (SSL), and port (443). We also need to bind a certificate, which can be done in the **SSL Settings** pane.

After we are done creating the load-balanced service, we need to make some changes in SharePoint. We have to configure public URLs under **Farm Settings** | **Alternate Access Mappings** in SharePoint. You can read more about this at http://technet.microsoft.com/en-us/library/cc263208.aspx. Now, we have successfully created a load-balanced SharePoint service.

Load balancing Lync 2013

Lync 2013 deployment consists of many different roles and services and is often quite complex compared to other Microsoft products, especially in conjunction with load balancing, since it uses many different protocols such as SIP and STUN and traditional protocols such as TCP and HTTPS.

Instead of covering the entire aspect of Lync deployment, I recommend you head on over to the deployment guide by Citrix available at `https://www.citrix.com/content/dam/citrix/en_us/documents/products-solutions/microsoft-lync-2013-and-citrix-netscaler-deployment-guide.pdf`.

Load balancing Exchange 2013

Exchange has always been difficult to load balance because of the way it works, but with the release of Exchange 2013, it has become a lot easier to load balance, as the architecture in Exchange 2013 has been dramatically simplified with only two roles, the **Client Access server** (**CAS**) and the Mailbox server. The CAS now only serves as a stateless proxy to the Mailbox server. This means that we can load balance on layer 4, as it does not matter which CAS a user is sent to. Also, RPC has been removed as a protocol, and now HTTPS is used by default with Outlook Anywhere, which makes it a lot easier to load balance. When configuring Exchange, we need to set up CAS using an external URL, which is available only via NetScaler.

With Exchange 2013 Service Pack 1, we also have the support do perform SSL offloading, but this is not configured by default and is not directly exposed in the Exchange management console. The advantage with performing SSL offloading is that we can use NetScaler to perform all the SSL transactions and therefore remove that processing from the CAS servers. This makes it certificate management easier as well. Also, another important thing to note is that if we upgrade our exchange environment, we must run the configuration change again after the update, since it by default reverts to non-SSL offloading.

We have a step-by-step guide on Microsoft TechNet describing how to configure SSL offloading on the different services, which is available at `https://technet.microsoft.com/en-us/library/dn635115(v=exchg.150).aspx`.

We can use the following script to enable SSL offloading for all services from within the Exchange PowerShell console:

```
Set-OutlookAnywhere -Identity MyServer\Rpc* -Externalhostname
MyServer.mail.contoso.com -ExternalClientsRequireSsl $True -
ExternalClientAuthenticationMethod Basic

Set-OutlookAnywhere -Identity MyServer\Rpc* -SSLOffloading $true
```

```
Set-WebConfigurationProperty -Filter //security/access -name sslflags
-Value "None" -PSPath IIS:  -Location "Default Web Site/OWA"
```

```
Set-WebConfigurationProperty -Filter //security/access -name sslflags
-Value "None" -PSPath IIS: -Location "Default Web Site/ecp"
```

```
Set-WebConfigurationProperty -Filter //security/access -name sslflags
-Value "None" -PSPath IIS: -Location "Default Web Site/EWS"
```

```
Set-WebConfigurationProperty -Filter //security/access -name sslflags
-Value "None" -PSPath IIS: -Location "Default Web Site/Autodiscover"
```

```
Set-WebConfigurationProperty -Filter //security/access -name sslflags
-Value "None" -PSPath IIS: -Location "Default Web Site/Microsoft-
Server-ActiveSync"
```

```
Set-WebConfigurationProperty -Filter //security/access -name sslflags
-Value "None" -PSPath IIS: -Location "Default Web Site/OAB"
```

```
Set-WebConfigurationProperty -Filter //security/access -name sslflags
-Value "None" -PSPath IIS: -Location "Default Web Site/MAPI"
```

```
iisreset /noforce
```

Now, with regard to the load-balancing capabilities, multiple features and protocols can be load balanced using NetScaler. They are listed as follows:

- **Outlook Web Access (OWA)**
- Outlook Anywhere
- ActiveSync
- IMAP4

OWA, Outlook Anywhere, and ActiveSync all use the same port and can be load balanced using the same vServer. The only difference is that they are available on different URL paths. First, we add the servers that are running as CAS to the list of servers. Next, we create a service or service group, which we will bind to the server on port 443 and protocol HTTPS. After we have chosen **HTTPS** as a protocol for the service, the **SSL Settings** pane will become active, and there we add the digitally signed certificate that is attached to CAS. This can be done by going to **Traffic Management | SSL**. From there, we can import the certificate, and then install it for the service.

 The purpose of the certificate is to ensure that NetScaler can enable a complete connection to the OWA server backend, as the use of the certificates requires that both parties have a trusted root certificate in place in order to trust the connection.

Next, we create a vServer to set up a load-balanced service. Then, we bind it to a virtual IP address, port (443), and protocol (SSL), and bind a new certificate to the vServer. Under **Method** and **Persistence**, we choose **Least Connection** and **COOKIEINSERT** respectively and a timeout of 2 minutes, and then click on **Create**. Also, it is important to set the external domain URL in CAS. This can be set from the Exchange management console, which you can read more about at `http://technet.microsoft.com/en-us/library/jj218640%28v=exchg.150%29.aspx`.

The external domain URL in the Exchange management console must point to the VIP address of the load-balanced service we created.

Load balancing IMAP on Exchange

IMAP is also a protocol that is commonly used in conjunction with Exchange, even though it does not provide many of the same features, such as calendar and public folders. IMAP is primarily used by a client to access e-mail on an Exchange server. Note that IMAP is not enabled by default on Exchange 2013. If you want to use this feature, you can read more about it at `http://technet.microsoft.com/en-us/library/bb124489(v=exchg.150).aspx`.

IMAP primarily uses two ports, TCP 143 for non-secure connections and TCP 993 for secure connections. Again, if we already have CAS on the server list, we do not need to add them again. If they are not added, add them to the list. Before we set up a service, we need to create a custom monitor. Go to **Traffic Management | Load Balancing | Monitors**, and click on **Add**. Enter a name, define an interval of 30 seconds, and define port 143 as the destination port. As type, choose **TCP-ECV** and then go to the **Special Parameters** pane. Here, type `The Microsoft Exchange IMAP4 service is ready` as the received string. This monitor queries CAS on that particular port and expects the text in response. Next, create a service or service group. Add CAS to the list and bind them to the service using protocol TCP and port 143. Then, bind the custom-made monitor we just created.

Now, create a vServer. To this, bind the service we created earlier, protocol `SSL_TCP`, port 993, and define a virtual IP address. Then, add a digital certificate in the **SSL Settings** pane of the vServer to ensure that clients can use the IMAP service securely.

Load balancing MSSQL

NetScaler is the only certified load balancer that can load balance MySQL and MSSQL services. It can be quite complex, and there are many requirements that need to be in place in order to set up a proper load-balanced SQL server.

Let's go through how to set up a load-balanced Microsoft SQL Server running on 2008 R2. It is important to remember that using load balancing between the end clients and SQL Server requires that the databases on the SQL server are synchronized. This is to ensure that the content that the user is requesting is available on all the backend servers. Microsoft SQL Server supports different types of availability solutions, such as replication. You can read more about it at `http://technet.microsoft.com/en-us/library/ms152565(v=sql.105).aspx`. Using transactional replication is recommended, as this replicates changes to different SQL servers as they occur.

> As of now, the load balancing solution for MSSQL, also called DataStream, supports only certain versions of SQL Server. They can be viewed at `http://support.citrix.com/proddocs/topic/netscaler-traffic-management-10-map/ns-dbproxy-reference-protocol-con.html`. Also, only certain authentication methods are supported. As of now, only SQL authentication is supported for MSSQL.

The steps to set up load balancing for MSSQL are as follows:

1. Add the backend SQL servers to the list of servers.

2. Next, create a custom monitor that we will use against the backend servers.

3. Before creating the monitor, we can create a custom database within SQL Server that NetScaler can query.

4. Open **Object Explorer** in the SQL Management Studio, and right-click on the **Database** folder. Then, select **New Database**, as shown in the following screenshot:

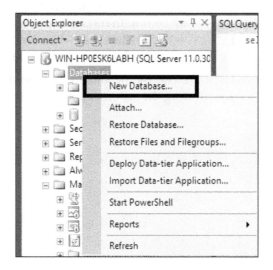

5. Name it ns and leave the rest at their default values; then click on **OK**. After that is done, go to the **Database** folder in **Object Explorer**.

6. Then, right-click on **Tables**, and click on **Create New Table**. Enter a column name (for example, test), and choose **nchar(10)** as the data type. Then, click on **Save Table**. This will present a dialog box that gives us the option to change the table name. Here, type test again.

7. We have now created a database called ns with a table called test, which contains a column that is also called test. This is an empty database that NetScaler will query to verify connectivity to the SQL server.

Now, we can go back to NetScaler and continue with the setup. First, we need to add a DBA user. This can be done by going to **System | User Administration | Database Users**, and clicking on **Add**. Enter a username and password for an SQL user who is allowed to log in and query the database.

After that is done, we can create a monitor. Go to **Traffic Management | Load Balancing | Monitors**, and click on **Add**. As the type, choose **MSSQL-ECV**, and then go to the **Special Parameters** pane.

Enter the following information:

*   **Database**: This is ns in this example.
*   **Query**: This is an SQL query that is run against the database. In our example, we type select * from test.
*   **User Name**: Here, we enter the name of the DBA user we created earlier. In our case, it is sa.
*   **Rule**: Here, we enter an expression that defines how NetScaler will verify whether the SQL server is up or not. In our example, it is MSSQL.RES. ATLEAST_ROWS_COUNT(0), which means that when NetScaler runs the query against the database, it should return zero rows from that table.
*   **Protocol Version**: Here, we choose the version that works with the SQL Server version we are running. In my case, it is SQL Server 2012.

So, the monitor now appears as in the following screenshot:

It is important that the database we created earlier is created on all the SQL servers we are going to load balance using NetScaler. So, now that we are done with the monitor, we can bind it to a service. When setting up the services against the SQL servers, remember to choose **MSSQL** as the protocol and 1433 as the port, and then bind the custom-made monitor to it. After that, we need to create a virtual load-balanced service. An important point to note here is that we choose **MSSQL** as the protocol and use the same port nr as we used before 1433.

Also, under the monitor, we have the ability to define if the monitor should store the databases that are stored in the backend, which is the StoreDB option in the monitor. This option is used if we want to perform specific database load balancing.

We can use NetScaler to proxy connections between different versions of SQL Server. As our backend servers are not set up to connect to the SQL 2012 version, we can present the vServer as a 2008 SQL server. For example, if we have an application that runs only against SQL Server 2005 for instance, we can make some custom changes to the vServer to make the NetScaler proxy in between. To create the load-balanced vServer, go to **Advanced | MSSQL | Server Version**. Here, we can choose different versions, as shown in the following screenshot:

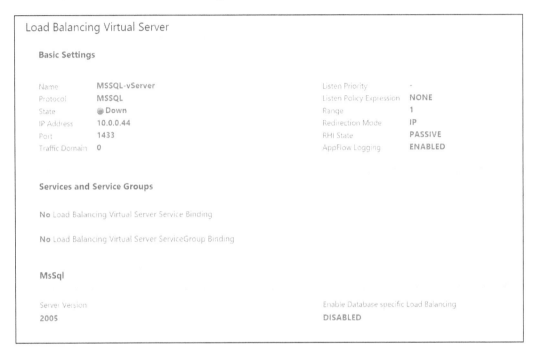

After we are done with the creation of the vServer, we can test it by opening a connection using the SQL Management Server to the VIP address. We can verify whether the connection is load balancing properly by running the following CLI command:

```
Stat lb vserver nameofvserver
```

Load balancing DNS

Load balancing DNS is not so much different from any regular service, and might also be needed to configure in case of setting up GSLB using NetScaler as a DNS Proxy.

There are, however, some settings that we need to be aware of. First, when we are setting up our services and need to bind a monitor to our backend DNS servers, we should create a custom monitor for DNS and enter a custom query to check if the DNS servers respond with the correct address. A custom monitor for DNS may look like the one in the following screenshot, where NetScaler will query the backend DNS server for an address; the IP addresses that return should match the values as shown in this screenshot:

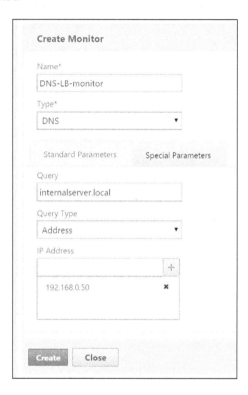

Second, when we set up the virtual load balancing server, we have some different options available for DNS under the basic settings of the vServer, which are as follows:

- **DNS64**: DNS64 needs to be enabled if you are having IPv6 clients that need to communicate with backend servers running IPv4. Also, this feature must be used in conjunction with NAT64.

- **Recursion Available**: This option is enabled when the backend servers that NetScaler is load balancing are set as recursive, which allows them to act as end resolvers for a DNS query.

- **Bypass AAAA requests**: If this option and DNS64 are enabled, NetScaler will not forward AAAA requests to the backend servers.

Persistency groups

In some cases, you might need to set up a load-balanced server based upon many different ports, and it is possible that a client needs to connect to that particular server using all the different ports. One scenario is RDP Gateway, which uses a mix of TCP 443 and UDP 3389; when an endpoint tries to connect to a server, we need to make sure that the client is redirected to the same gateway server instead of being redirected to another server on the other port. This is where persistency groups come in: they allow us to create a group of persisted connections against the same server.

To create persistency groups, navigate to **Traffic Management | Load Balancing | Persistency Groups** and click on **Add**. From here, give it a name and choose **Persistency Type**, and then add the servers that should be a part of the same group, as shown in the following screenshot:

Summary

In this chapter, we went through the different load-balanced services, such as a generic web application, different Citrix components, Exchange, SharePoint, and SQL Server using the DataStream service. Load balancing is essential for many businesses, and it is important to understand how NetScaler can load balance between different backend servers.

In the next chapter, we will cover the mobilestream feature of Citrix, and how we can use this feature to optimize web services using compression, caching, and so forth.

4
Mobilestream

Mobilestream is a set of features on NetScaler that, in essence, optimizes traffic going back to endpoints. This chapter will focus on three of its features: compression, caching, and frontend optimization. The following topics will be covered in this chapter:

- What is mobilestream?
- What is caching?
- What is compression?
- What is frontend optimization?
- How do they work?
- How to configure mobilestream for web services

NetScaler Mobilestream, as I mentioned, is a set of key features in NetScaler that enhances service delivery to mobile devices. However, in essence, it's a marketing term that combines features such as TCP optimization and application firewall—which are both subjects that we will cover in a later chapter—but it also contains features such as frontend optimization, compression, and caching, which are more HTTP-based application features. Let's explore what these features are and how they work:

- **Compression**: This is the ability to reduce the number of bits within data. More specifically, it is the ability to use fewer bits than in the original data, as it is compressed.

- **Caching**: This allows for a NetScaler unit to store commonly accessed data in the RAM, which allows for quicker fetching of data.

- **Frontend optimization**: This allows NetScaler to perform smart data changes to web content such as CSS, PNG, JS, HTML, and such. For instance, it can resize and convert image based upon endpoint connecting.

All these three features allow the client to get hold of the content faster, as they save bandwidth between the service and the client. They can also reduce traffic to backend servers and protect the backend servers from traffic storms. An important point to note is that these features are not included by default in the standard edition of NetScaler. In order to use these features, we either need to buy a feature license or upgrade to the Enterprise or Platinum edition. In order to use caching, we must upgrade to either NetScaler Platinum or NetScaler Enterprise and then buy a feature license.

So, let's start by taking a look at the compression feature of NetScaler.

Compression

The compression feature enables a NetScaler vServer to compress HTTP data that is going to or from the client. Another benefit of this feature is that the HTTP compression algorithm encrypts the data going from the client to the server and therefore adds another layer of security.

 Using compression does not encrypt the data as efficiently as using a digitally signed certificate, so do not contemplate replacing certificates with compression.

The compression feature requires that the client who is requesting the content have a browser that supports compression. The newest and most common browsers, such as Firefox 4 and above, Google Chrome 20 and above, and Internet Explorer 7 and above, support HTTP compression. So, when a client connects to a vServer, it will announce what capabilities it has to the server. This allows NetScaler to choose the best type of algorithm.

 HTTP compression is based on the GZIP and DEFLATE algorithms. These are defined in RFC 1950/1951/1952 formats. Those interested in its technical aspects may read more at http://www.ietf.org/rfc/rfc1952.txt.

Now, the HTTP compression feature of NetScaler will compress data within HTML, XML, CSS, text, and Microsoft Office documents. It does not compress any picture format files, JavaScript files, or other web files that are not text related.

In order to configure compression in NetScaler, first enable the feature globally in the appliance. This can be done using the following CLI command:

```
enable ns feature cmp
```

Here, `cmp` stands for compression. After enabling this feature in NetScaler, activate it for a service. A service in this context can be a load-balanced service. This can be done using the following CLI command:

```
Set service nameofservice -CMP yes
```

This can also be done through the GUI under **Traffic Management**. Then, click on **Service** and go to the **Advanced** pane. Navigate to the **Settings** section of the window and enable **Compression**, as shown in the following screenshot:

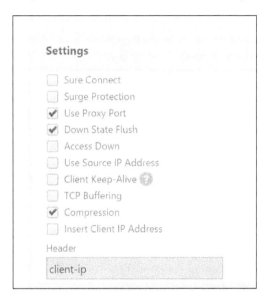

 Using Wireshark to analyze network traffic using filters and the different types of HTTP headers will be covered as part of *Chapter 7, Security and Troubleshooting*.

Implementing compression policies

Now, after compression has been enabled, NetScaler will use the default policies that are set at a global level. We can see that after we enable compression for a service, it will automatically start compressing data for that service. If we go to the HTTP **Compression Policy Manager** window under **HTTP Compression** and then choose Override Global and click Continue, we will be able to see the policies that are applied on a global level.

The reason why we need to go for the classic syntax here is that in the global settings of the compression feature, we have a configuration that defines which policies are processed and which are not. By default, this is configured to be of the Classic policy type. This policy is covered later in this chapter.

By default, there are five global policies, each of which has an action attached to it. The policies are explained as follows:

- ns_nocmp_xml_ie: This policy does not compress when a request is sent from Internet Explorer. The content type is either text or XML.

- ns_nocmp_mozilla_47: This policy does not compress when a request is sent from Firefox. The content type is either text or XML.

- ns_cmp_mscss: This policy compresses the CSS file when the request is sent from Internet Explorer.

- ns_cmp_msapp: This policy compresses files that are generated by Microsoft Word, Excel, or PowerPoint.

- ns_cmp_content_type: This policy compresses data when the response contains text.

These policies can be seen in the following screenshot:

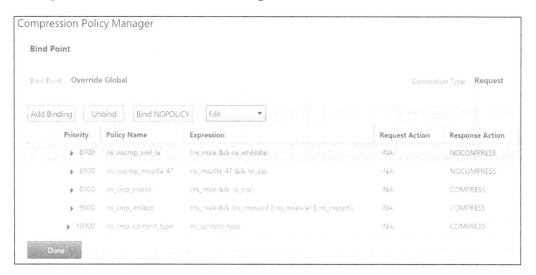

These policies do not compress data coming from the client to the services, but they compress data that is generated from the servers, which contains CSS files, Microsoft Office documents, or text.

After we have enabled compression for a service, we can test it by running a few HTTP requests against a service, for example, by opening a web browser to a service we defined in NetScaler. In my example, I have a simple IIS server setup, where I query the index page.

To view statistics, use the following CLI command:

```
Show cmp stats
```

We can also go through the GUI under **HTTP Compression | Statistics**, as shown in the following screenshot:

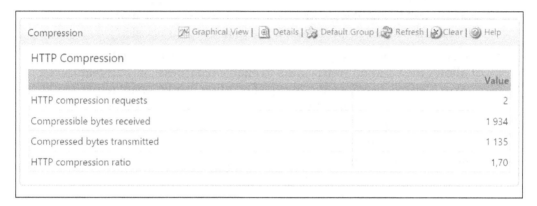

We can see that it has already managed to compress about 50 percent of the data. This feature uses the CPU of the appliance. So make sure that you do not enable compression if you have a large number of services, as NetScaler uses a large amount of CPU to perform compression.

Defining global compression settings

We can define some global settings to make sure that the compression feature does not run if NetScaler exceeds a particular amount of CPU usage. To do this, go to **Optimization | HTTP Compression | Settings | Change Compression Settings**. Here, define the following parameters:

- **Quantum Size**: This parameter defines the amount of data that has to go through before NetScaler starts to compress data. The default value here is 57,344 or 57 KB.

- **Compression Level**: Here, we can define at what level NetScaler should compress data. Best performance equals less compression and less CPU usage. Best compression equals more CPU usage.

- **Minimum HTTP Response Size**: This parameter defines what the minimum size of an HTTP response must be before it starts to compress. This should be set at a minimum of 100 KB so that NetScaler does not use a lot of CPU to compress small responses.

- **Bypass Compression On CPU Usage**: Here, we can define a percentage of CPU usage before NetScaler bypasses the compression feature. By default, this is set at 100 percent, which means that if NetScaler has 100 percent CPU usage, the compression feature is bypassed.

- **Policy Type**: Here, we can define a classic policy or an advanced policy. When we enable compression at a global level, it means that all classic policies will be enabled. If we create an advanced policy and bind it globally, it will not be processed if the policy type is classic.

- **Allow Server-side Compression**: If we have this feature enabled, it allows the backend web servers to enable compression. This feature makes NetScaler remove the Accept-Encoding header on all requests going to the web server, which makes the web server respond with an uncompressed response. This makes NetScaler respond to the client with a compressed response.

- **Compress Push Packet**: This allows NetScaler to avoid waiting until it reaches the quantum size before it can start to compress data when it receives a TCP packet with the PUSH flag enabled.

- **Vary Header**: This feature adds the Vary header to HTTP responses that are being compressed. This is mostly used in caching scenarios.

- **External Cache**: If private caching is enabled, NetScaler will add private cache-control to the HTTP header to make sure that the data is intended for a single user.

Now, most of these settings will be at their default values, but if you have a scenario where you, for example, have lots of large services and web servers with backend-enabled compression, you will need to change some settings here to make sure that it works properly. Another adjustment might be to change the bypass compression CPU usage feature, since you never want to be in a situation where NetScaler is at 100 percent CPU.

Creating custom compression policies

We have gone through the different settings; it is now time to create our own compression policies. A policy is built up of a rule and an action. The rule can contain a query, for example, a client who is connecting using Firefox version 4.7. The default action for this rule would be to compress data.

Follow these steps to create a compression policy:

1. Go to **Optimization | HTTP Compression | Policies | Add**.

2. Next, add an expression in the **Expression** window. Note that you can choose from a list of predefined expressions.

3. As an example, choose **Saved Policy Expressions** and select **ns_msie**, and add the **Compress** action.

4. The expression should be similar to the one shown in the following screenshot:

5. If you choose **Expression Editor** here, you can define a custom expression based upon the URL, header, IP, and so on. I'm not going to cover all the different types of expressions that can be used. Citrix has a good overview of the different expressions that can be used in classic syntax at `https://docs.citrix.com/en-us/netscaler/11/reference/netscaler-advanced-policy-expression-reference.html`.

6. After creating the policy, either bind the policy to a service or bind it globally. Go to **HTTP Compression Policy Manager | Override Global**. Then, click on **Add Binding** and select the newly created policy. Note that the policy gets a priority, which places it lower than the other inbuilt policies.

An important point to note is that classic and default syntaxes can perform the same type of evaluations, but the default syntax policies can also analyze deeper within the data, for example, the body of a HTTP request. It is therefore recommended to start using default syntax policies.

Testing our compression policies

To test a policy against a service, bind it to the service and define a low-numbered priority to make sure that it applies before other policies. In this example, we've added the newly created policy to the global level, and set it at priority 100 so that we can make sure that the policy is applied to all connections made from Internet Explorer. We can also unbind all the other policies to make sure that no other policies interfere with the one for Internet Explorer.

So, when we try to open a connection from Internet Explorer, we will be able to see from the packets that the traffic is compressed from the HTTP request header. We can see this in the following screenshot in the **Content-Encoding** field, which says it is compressed with **gzip**:

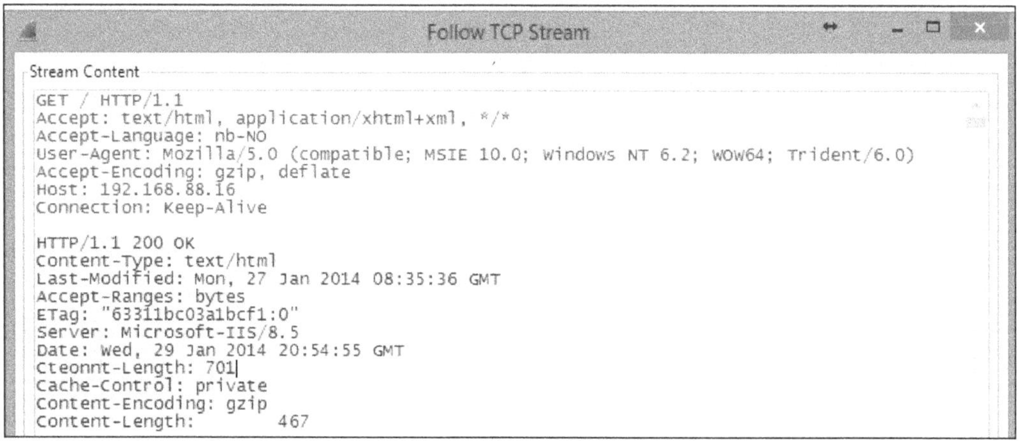

If we do the same for Google Chrome and analyze the traffic in Wireshark, we can see in the following screenshot that the traffic is not compressed and the data is sent in clear text, as there is no policy that involves an expression containing an action for Google Chrome:

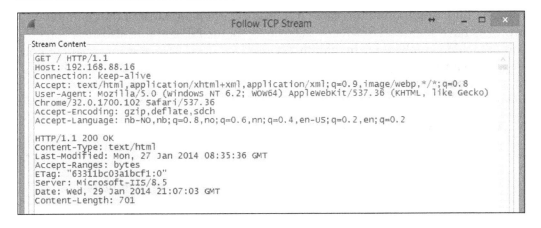

We have now created a custom policy for Internet Explorer users and explored the different options for compression and how it works. We can verify if the compression policies are working by going into **HTTP Compression | Policies**. This will list out all our policies and show the current hits of the policy and the bandwidth savings of the different policies, as seen in the following screenshot:

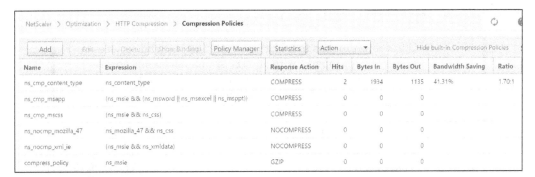

Name	Expression	Response Action	Hits	Bytes In	Bytes Out	Bandwidth Saving	Ratio
ns_cmp_content_type	ns_content_type	COMPRESS	2	1934	1135	41.31%	1.70:1
ns_cmp_msapp	(ns_msie && (ns_msword || ns_msexcel || ns_msppt))	COMPRESS	0	0	0		
ns_cmp_mscss	(ns_msie && ns_css)	COMPRESS	0	0	0		
ns_nocmp_mozilla_47	ns_mozilla_47 && ns_css	NOCOMPRESS	0	0	0		
ns_nocmp_xml_ie	(ns_msie && ns_xmldata)	NOCOMPRESS	0	0	0		
compress_policy	ns_msie	GZIP	0	0	0		

Caching

By using caching, we allow NetScaler to store frequently accessed objects in its cache area, which uses the RAM of the appliance as storage. Note that the MPX utilizes the SSD drive as the cache drive. This allows NetScaler to serve clients directly without requiring a trip to the backend servers. This offloads the backend servers and improves the overall performance of the services.

Now, caching is not something new; it is used everywhere. Most of the common web browsers have some sort of a local cache; many of the ISP vendors also have some sort of caching involved for frequently accessed services. Also, it is important to note that this feature requires a license to be in place, either a NetScaler Platinum license, or an add-on to Enterprise. Note that the caching feature is available only when using the HTTP protocol, and it can cache the following two types of data content:

- **Static data**: This includes CSS files, JavaScript files, images, static HTML pages, and so on. Static data is now being used in conjunction with frontend optimization.

- **Dynamic data**: This includes the dynamic catalog view, automatically generated files, and so on.

Enabling caching

Before we process any configuration, we first need to enable the caching feature. This can either be done via the GUI by right-clicking on **Integrated Caching** under **Optimization** and enabling this feature, or by using the following CLI command:

```
Enable ns feature IC
```

 Citrix recommends that NetScaler and the backend services be time-synced properly with an NTP source, since this ensures that content and caching work better instead of storing older data, or if used with the pre-fetch feature.

Before we do any other configuration, we also need to define some of the global settings for caching. This can be done under **Optimization | Integrated Caching | Change Cache Settings**. After we have enabled integrated caching, the default value for memory usage limit is set to 0, which means that NetScaler will not cache anything. Therefore, we need to put a value here. The maximum value that we can set is half of the memory available on the appliance. After we have put a value here, we can leave the rest of the settings at their default values and continue with the creation of a policy.

The caching feature consists of the following:

- A policy
- An action
- A content group

In the policy, we define an expression (rule) that needs to be evaluated, and then an action that defines what to do with the data defined in the rule, for example, to cache the objects or not. Then, we define a content group. This is where NetScaler is going to store the cached data for the objects.

 In a deployment with multiple packet engines, all the PEs have access to the cache and are aware of what kind of content is in the cache via a shared memory table.

Creating a content group

As an example, let's set up a basic caching policy that caches PDF files. Then, we will bind that policy to a load-balanced service.

First, we need to create a content group. This can be done by going to **Optimization | Integrated Caching | Content Groups** and clicking on **Add**. Here, we enter the name of the content group, for example, PDF group. Then we define **Type** to be **HTTP**, define an expiration timer (60 seconds), and then go into the **Memory** pane and define that NetScaler does not have to cache if the file exceeds 5,000 KB. By adding these parameters, we allow cached content to live in the content group for 60 seconds before it expires and then be removed from the content group. We also define that NetScaler should not cache objects larger than 5 MB. We can leave the rest of the settings at their default values.

If you wish to know more about the different parameters in the content group, you can view the eDocs article at `https://docs.citrix.com/en-us/netscaler/11/optimization/integrated-caching/configuring-selectors-basic-content-groups/setting-up-basic-content-group.html`.

Creating a caching policy

Now that we have created a content group, we can create a policy. Go to **Policies** and click on **Add**. Now, we need to define an expression that only includes PDF files, attach an action, and configure where NetScaler is going to store the files. Give the policy a name, choose **CACHE** as the action, change **Store in Group**, and choose the content group that was created earlier.

In the **Expressions** field, type the expression `HTTP.REQ.URL.ENDSWITH("pdf")`. This expression allows NetScaler to cache all objects where the URL ends with `pdf`. We could also use the `HTTP.REQ.URL.CONTAINS(\"pdf\")` expression if we had pages containing links to PDF reports.

If you wish to combine multiple expressions in a policy, you can see the example at `https://docs.citrix.com/en-us/netscaler/11/optimization/integrated-caching/configuring-policies-caching-invalidation/integrated-cache-policy-configuration.html`. After we have added the expression, the window will look like the following screenshot:

Lastly, click on **Create**. Now that we have created the policy, we have to bind it to the vServer, for which we want caching enabled. Go to the **Integrated Caching** menu and open **Cache Policy Manager**. Change bindpoint to Load Balanced Virtual Server and choose the load-balanced vServer to bind it to. Then click on **Continue**, choose **Select Policy** and find the newly created policy. We have now created a caching policy and attached it to a vServer, which has a PDF document available. When the first client connects to the vServer and tries to get the content, NetScaler will place it in the cache.

This can be viewed under **Integrated Caching | Statistics**, as shown in the following screenshot:

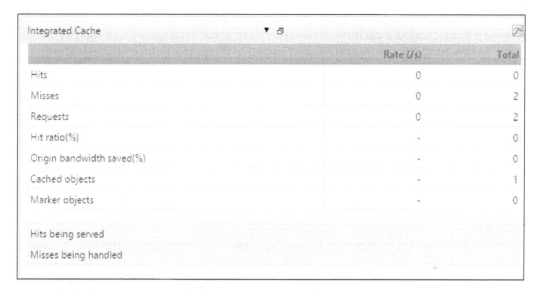

As this is the first connection, we will see a Miss and one Cached object. If we go to **Integrated Caching | View Cache Objects | All**, we can see what data is stored in the cache. We can also see that the PDF file is stored in the content group we defined earlier, as shown in the following screenshot:

As we can see from the statistics in the following screenshot, when a new client connects, it will be served from the cache directly, thus allowing us to save bandwidth:

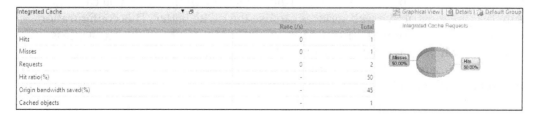

A new client will be allowed to get data from the cache as long as the content it is trying to access has not expired. If we open an object from within **View Cache Objects**, we can see how much time an object has before it expires.

After we have created a caching policy, there are some settings we can modify in order to fine-tune the configuration and improve the performance of this feature.

Fine-tuning caching

One problem with caching occurs when multiple users try to access the same data simultaneously and NetScaler has not finished downloading the object into the cache. This leaves the cache in a state where multiple users are directed to the backend servers instead of the cache.

There are some changes we need to make to ensure that clients do not bypass the cache. These are explained as follows:

- **Prefetch**: This allows NetScaler to refresh the content before the object expires.
- **Flash Cache**: When a large number of users try to access the same content, NetScaler sends only one connection to the backend server, and all subsequent requests are queued up. A single response is used to respond to all the users.

Both these settings can be configured in the content group, which stores the cached objects. We can do this by opening a content group, and going to **Others | Flash Crowd | Prefetch**. Here, we can define both these values within the group. Under **Prefetch**, we define how often NetScaler should evaluate the objects in the cache and check the expiration and how often it should refresh the cache. In the same pane, we can also see the active flash cache.

There are, of course, other configurations that we can set to improve the caching mechanism. By default, when we set up a cache policy, it will cache everything that is picked up by the rule.

If you have multiple load-balanced services and you have caching enabled, the cache space will fill up quickly. There are, of course, some web services that are more frequently accessed than others, so you do not want the less-accessed resources to fill up the cache space. You can attach a rule that defines the minimum number of requests to a server before the caching rule is enabled. In this way, you can make sure that the most active web services can use the cache better. This configuration can be set under **Content Group | Memory | Do Not Cache**, if the hits are less. The number here is again dependent on the amount of traffic going towards the different web services. If you are unsure about the amount of traffic going to the different vServers and services, use CLI commands.

For services, use the following CLI command:

`Stat service servicename`

For vServers, use the following CLI command:

`Stat lb vserver vservername`

This gives you a general idea of where to set the hit rate of objects that have been fetched from the cache.

 If you are unsure of the prefix on a CLI command, you can use the *Tab* key. For example, if you type `stat` and press the *Tab* key, you will get a list of the available options.

It is important to note that you can use the compression feature with the caching feature. This enables NetScaler to send compressed data from the cache to the clients that support compression.

If you want to see a graphical overview of the policies and their statistics for a vServer, you can check the visualizer feature by right-clicking on a vServer in the NetScaler GUI and choosing **Visualizer**. This can be seen in the following screenshot:

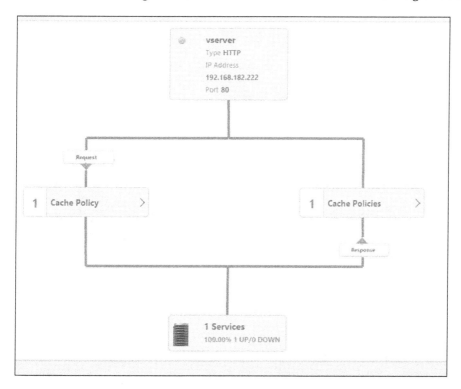

Here, you can choose filters based upon what you want to display in the GUI. If you choose **Caching** and **Compression** from the top pane, you will be able to see what policies are attached to the vServer. Also, you can view statistics for a policy by marking it. This is a good way to see what policies are actually attached to a vServer and what their statistics are.

Frontend optimization

Most websites today consist of a huge piece of CSS that contains style sheets that define how a website should look. Many have JavaScript to make the website more dynamic. Many sites are also media-heavy, meaning that they have a large amount of image and video content. A common problem with these sites that they are not always optimized for mobile users in terms of delivery.

This is where frontend optimization comes in—it allows NetScaler to optimize data before sending it back to the client.

So what can frontend optimization actually do? Here's a list:

- JavaScript
  - Make inline
  - Minify

- Image
  - Shrink to attributes
  - Convert GIF to PNG
  - Lazy load
  - Make inline
  - Optimize
  - Convert to WEBP
  - Convert to the JXR format

- CSS
  - Make inline
  - Combine
  - Convert imports to links
  - Minify
  - Image inline

- HTML
    - ° Remove comments from HTML

- Domain sharding

Some of these are self-explanatory, but some require some more description, for instance, image lazy loading. When loading a website on a mobile device, it is common that the mobile device browser loads the entire website into buffer before the website is displayed for the user. For a website containing multiple images, it might take some time, and the user might not even be interested in looking at all the images on the page.

Image lazy load is a JavaScript feature that allows the images to be loaded to the client when the user is scrolling down the webpage.

Domain sharding is a feature that allows us to overcome the limitations of the HTTP 1.1 protocol. By default, most web browsers can only open a certain number of connections to the same domain—domain sharding tries to overcome this limitation by splitting the connections on multiple domains.

It is important to remember that frontend optimization works in conjunction with the caching feature. When we have a frontend policy applied, NetScaler will start parsing the content of a request, create an entry in the cache, apply the frontend policy, and then store the optimized content in the cache entry. Then for subsequent requests, content will be served from the cache and not from the server.

To set up frontend optimization, we must create a policy that contains an expression and actions on what to optimize. By default, NetScaler has five built-in policies, BASIC, MODERATE, AGGRESSIVE, IMG_OPTIMIZE, and NONE. All these policies have the different actions that we described earlier.

We also have the option to create our own actions. We can do this by going into **Optimization | Front End Optimization | Actions**, then clicking on **Add** and defining which feature we want to activate.

After we have created an ACTION, we will need to create a policy that references it. Now, it may not be effective to have different actions applied for regular desktop-based users. Therefore, we could scope this policy to just apply it for Android-based users, for instance. So when creating a policy, we reference the actions and use an expression to include Android, using a regular HTTP REQ expression, as shown in the following screenshot:

After we have created a policy, we need to bind it to a virtual server. Navigate to **Virtual Server | Profiles | Choose Front End optimization**, type request, and click on **Continue**. Choose the newly-created frontend policy and click on **Select**. After the policy has been added, the statistics can be viewed.

For instance, if we go back to the **Front End Optimization** menu, we have an option called **Statistics**. This will give us an overview of the statistics for the frontend feature and will display, for instance, how many images have been resized, how much data has been saved, and so on.

Summary

We have now configured compression, caching, and frontend optimization for NetScaler. All these features provide a drastic improvement in web services, if properly configured. They may use more CPU and memory in NetScaler. So, you need to plan properly.

In the next chapter, we will go deeper into optimization, and even deeper into TCP tuning and SSL.

Optimizing NetScaler Traffic

5

The purpose of NetScaler is to act as a logistics department. It has to serve content to many different endpoints using many different protocols across different types of media, and it can either be a physical device or on top of a hypervisor within a private cloud infrastructure. Since there are many factors that play in here, there is room for tuning and improvement. Some of the topics we will cover in this chapter are:

- Tuning for virtual environments
- Tuning TCP traffic
- Tuning SSL traffic
- HTTP/2 and SPDY
- Other network capabilities

Tuning for virtual environments

When setting up NetScaler in a virtual environment, there are many factors that affect how it might perform. For instance, the underlying CPUs of the virtual host, NIC throughput and capabilities, vCPU over allocation, NIC teaming, MTU size, and so on. So, it is always important to remember the hardware requirements when setting up NetScaler VPX on a virtualization host.

Another important factor when setting up NetScaler VPX is the concept of Package Engines. By default, when we set up or import NetScaler, it is set up with two vCPUs. The first of these two are dedicated for management purposes, and the second vCPU is dedicated to doing all the packet processing, such as content switching, SSL offloading, ICA-proxy, and so on.

It is important to note that the second vCPU might be seen as 100% utilized in the hypervisor performance monitoring tools, but the correct way to check if it is being utilized is by using the CLI-command stat system.

Now, by default, VPX 10 and VPX 200 only have support for one packet engine. This is because of the bandwidth limitations, it does not require more packet engine CPUs to process the packets. On the other hand, VPX 1000 and VPX 3000 have support for up to three packet engines. This is in most cases needed to process all the packets that are going through the system if the bandwidth is going to be utilized to its fullest.

In order to add a new packet engine, we need to assign more vCPUs and memory to the VPX. Packet engines also have the benefit of load balancing processing between them. So, instead of having a vCPU that is 100% utilized, we can even the load between multiple vCPUs and get even better performance and bandwidth. The following is a chart that shows the different editions and support for multiple packet engines:

License/Memory	2 GB	4 GB	6 GB	8 GB	10 GB	12 GB
VPX 10	1	1	1	1	1	1
VPX 200	1	1	1	1	1	1
VPX 1000	1	2	3	3	3	3
VPX 3000	1	2	3	3	3	3

It is important to remember that multiple PE are only available for VMware, XenServer, and Hyper-V, and not for KVM.

If we plan on using NIC-teaming on the underlying virtualization host, there are some important aspects to consider.

Most of the different vendors have guidelines that describe the kind of load balancing techniques that are available in the hypervisor.

For instance, Microsoft has a guide here that describes their features
`http://www.microsoft.com/en-us/download/details.aspx?id=30160`.

One of the NIC teaming options called Switch Independent Dynamic Mode has an interesting side effect in that it replaces the source MAC address of the virtual machine with one of the primary NICs on the host, and, therefore, we might experience packet loss on a VPX. Therefore, it is recommended in most cases that we have LACP/LAG, or in case of Hyper-V, use the Hyper-V Port distribution feature instead.

Features such as SRV-IO or PCI pass-through are not supported for NetScaler VPX.

NetScaler 11 also introduced the support for Jumbo Frames for the VPX. This allows for a much higher payload in an Ethernet frame. Instead of the traditional 1,500 bytes, we can scale up to 9,000 bytes of payload. This allows for a much lower overhead since the frames contain more data.

This requires that the underlying NIC on the hypervisor supports this feature and is enabled as well, and this in most cases just works for communication with backend resources and not with users accessing public resources. This is because most routers and ISP block such high MTU.

This feature can be configured at the Interface level in NetScaler, which can be done under **System | Network | Interface**. Choose and select interface and click on **Edit**. Here, we have the option called Maximum Transmission Unit, which can be adjusted up to 9,216 bytes.

It is important to note that NetScaler can communicate with backend resources using Jumbo frames and then adjust the MTU when communicating back with clients. It can also communicate with Jumbo frames in both paths, in case NetScaler is set up as a backend load balancer.

It is also important to note that NetScaler only supports Jumbo frames load balancing for the following protocols:

- TCP
- TCP-based protocols such as HTTP
- SIP
- RADIUS

TCP tuning

Much of the traffic that is going through NetScaler is based on the TCP protocol. Either it is ICA-Proxy, HTTP, or something similar.

TCP is a protocol that provides a reliable, error-checked delivery of packets back and forth. This ensures that data is successfully transferred before being processed further. TCP has many features to adjust bandwidth during transfer, congestion checking, adjusting segment sizing, and so on, which we will delve into a bit in this section.

As mentioned in an earlier chapter, we can adjust the way NetScaler uses TCP using TCP profiles. By default, all services and vServers that are created on the NetScaler use the default TCP profile `nstcp_default_profile`.

These profiles can be found under **System | Profiles | TCP Profiles**. Make sure not to alter the default TCP profile without properly consulting the network team, as this affects the way TCP works for all default services on NetScaler.

This default profile has most of the different TCP features turned off. This is to ensure compatibility with most infrastructures. The profile has not been adjusted much since it was first added in NetScaler. Citrix also has a lot of other different profiles depending on the use cases. So we will look a bit closer at the different options we have here.

For instance, the profile `nstcp_default_XA_XD_profile`, which is intended for ICA-proxy traffic, has some differences from the default profile:

- Window Scaling
- Selective Acknowledgement
- Forward Acknowledgement
- Use of Nagles Algorithm

Window Scaling is a TCP option that allows the receiving point to accept more data than is allowed in the TCP RFC for window size before getting an acknowledgment. By default, the window size is set to accept 65.536 bytes. With Window scaling enabled, it basically shifts the window size bitwise. This is a option that needs to be enabled on both endpoints in order to be used, and will only be sent in the initial three-way handshake.

Select Acknowledgement (SACK) is a TCP option that allows for better handling of TCP retransmission. In a scenario where there are two hosts communicating with SACK not enabled, and suddenly one of the hosts drops out of the network, it loses some packets when it comes back online and receives more packets from the other host. In this case, the first host will ACK from the last packet it got from the other host before it dropped out. With SACK enabled, it will notify the other host of the last packet it got before it dropped out, and the other packets it received when it went back online. This allows for faster recovery of the communication, since the other host does not need to resend all the packets.

Forward Acknowledgement (FACK) is a TCP option that works in conjunction with SACK that helps avoid TCP congestion by measuring the total number of data bytes outstanding in the network. Using the information from SACK, it can more precisely calculate how much data it can retransmit.

Nagles Algorithm is a TCP feature that tries to cope with the small packet problem. Applications such as Telnet often send each keystroke within its own packet, creating multiple small packets containing only 1 byte of data, which results in a 41-byte packet for one keystroke. The algorithm works by combining a number of small outgoing messages into the same message, thus avoiding any overhead.

Since ICA is a protocol that operates with many small packets that might create congestion, Nagle is enabled in the TCP profile. Also, since many might be connecting using 3G or Wi-Fi, which might in some cases be unreliable to change channel, we need options that require the clients to be able to re-establish a connection fast, allowing the use of SACK and FACK.

Note that Nagle might have negative performance on applications that have their own buffering mechanism and operate inside LAN.

If we take a look at another profile, such as `nstcp_default_lan`, we can see that FACK is disabled. This is because the resources needed to calculate the amount of outstanding data in a high-speed network might be too much.

Another important aspect of these profiles are the TCP congestion algorithms. For instance, `nstcp_default_mobile` uses the Westwood congestion algorithm. This is because it is much better at handling large bandwidth-delay paths, such as wireless.

The following congestion algorithms are available in NetScaler:

- Default (based on TCP Reno)
- Westwood (based on TCP Westwood+)
- BIC
- CUBIC
- Nile (based on TCP Illinois)

What is worth noting here is that Westwood is aimed at 3G/4G connections, or other slow wireless connections. BIC is aimed at high bandwidth connections with high latency, such as WAN connections. CUBIC is almost like BIC but not as aggressive when it comes to fast-ramp and retransmissions. It is important to note, however, is that CUBIC is the default TCP algorithm in Linux kernels from 2.6.19 to 3.1

Nile, which is a newly created algorithm created by Citrix, is based on TCP Illinois, which is targeted at high-speed, long-distance networks. It achieves a higher throughput than standard TCP and is also compatible with standard TCP.

So, here we can customize which algorithm is better suited to a service. For instance, if we have a vServer that serves content to mobile devices, we could use the `nstcp_default_mobile` TCP profile.

There are also some other parameters that are important to think about in the TCP profile.

One of these parameters is multipath TCP. This is a feature that allows an endpoint to have multiple paths to a service. This is typically a mobile device that has WLAN and 3G capabilities, and allows the device to communicate with a service on NetScaler using both channels at the same time. This requires that the device supports communication on both methods and that the service or application on the device supports Multipath TCP.

So, let's take an example of what a TCP profile might look like if we have a vServer on NetScaler that is used to service an application to mobile devices. This means the most common way that users can access this service is by using 3G or Wi-Fi. The web service has its own buffering mechanism, which means it tries not to send small packets over the link. The application is Multipath-TCP aware.

In this scenario, we could leverage the `nstcp_default_mobile` profile, since it has most of the defaults for a mobile scenario, but we could also enable multipath TCP and create a new profile of it, and bind it to the vServer.

In order to bind a TCP profile to a vServer, navigate to the particular vServer, then **Edit** | **Profiles** | **TCP Profiles**, as shown in the following screenshot:

AOL did a presentation of their own TCP customization on NetScaler. You can take a look at the presentation at `http://www.slideshare.net/masonke/net-scaler-tcpperformancetuningintheaol network`. It is important to note that TCP should always be done in cooperation with the network team.

SSL tuning

Now, another important piece of tuning the traffic is tuning how NetScaler should handle encrypted traffic. However, one important aspect to think about is that the higher the encryption levels go, the slower the throughput gets.

This means the best performance does not always give the best performance; therefore, it is always important to think what is the necessary level of security before starting to tune SSL.

Nevertheless, we will be discussing some of the SSL features that can be tuned.

On NetScaler, we have something called SSL profiles that allow us to define how SSL traffic should be handled. These profiles can then be bound to a vServer or Service depending on the requirements. Now, unlike TCP profiles, we need to define whether an SSL profile should be frontend or backend, as shown in the following screenshot:

This is because NetScaler has different capabilities, depending on whether the communication is public facing or whether it is going to a backend server.

The SSL profiles is located under the same menu as the TCP profile, that is, **System** | **Profiles** | **SSL Profile**.

The first thing we should take a look at in the SSL profile is the quantum size. This parameter defines how much data in KB should be processed before it is encrypted. By default, this value is at 8,192 KB. If we are hosting a service that provides media downloads, for instance, or large files in general, we would get a benefit if we changed this to a larger quantum size.

Another feature is the Push encryption trigger. By default, this value is used to tell NetScaler how long it should wait before consolidating the data and encrypting it.

For instance, ICA-proxy sessions have the PSH flag set, which means that NetScaler should always forward encrypted traffic without delay. If we set this value to 5 ms, NetScaler will gather data for 5 ms before sending it back to the client.

By default, this value is set to 1 ms. In an environment with a lot of ICA-proxy sessions, the network might be congested because of the high amount of small packets that need to be encapsulated.

Another important aspect of the SSL profile is determining which protocol to use. By default, an SSL-based vServer can communicate with SSL 3, TLS 1, TLS 1.1, and TLS 1.2.

As a recommendation, SSL 3 and TLS 1 should always be turned off because of security risks. Most clients and browsers today support the use of TLS 1.1 and 1.2.

Another aspect of SSL is which kind of ciphers to use. These ciphers decide which kind of protocol to use, as well as what kind of encryption algorithm, key exchange algorithm, and what kind of message authentication code algorithm to use.

The different ciphers can be found under **Traffic Management | SSL | Cipher Groups**. In this eDocs article at `http://docs.citrix.com/en-us/netscaler/10-5/ns-tmg-wrapper-10-con/ns-ssl-wrapper-con-10/ns-ssl-supported-ciphers-list-ref.html`, we can see all the different ciphers that work with the different protocols. Depending on our security requirements, we should decide which ciphers should be available for our service. For instance, RSA is faster than DH, but it's less secure. RC4 encryption is faster than AES 256, but is less secure.

We can get more information regarding our SSL capabilities at `https://www.howsmyssl.com/`.

The different cipher groups are not part of an SSL profile and need to be adjusted for each vServer. It can be done either using specific ciphers or we can choose specific cipher groups, as shown in the following screenshot:

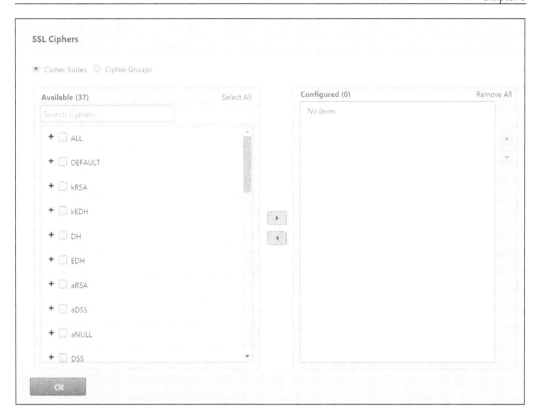

HTTP/2 and SPDY

So far, we have discussed the lower layers of the ISO model with SSL, TCP, and Ethernet capabilities. The last piece of this puzzle is the application layer. This is where HTTP/2 and SPDY come in.

Now, HTTP 1.1 is the de facto standard of the Web, it has been around for 11 years and is not optimized for today's Internet.

Over the years, Google has done a lot of work trying to improve this web protocol. The company got as far as creating its own protocol, which was called SPDY. This protocol uses prioritizing and connection multiplexing, which allows the communication flow to go a lot faster. It also has the transmission headers sent using GZIP or deflate, and since the headers are sent in a binary format instead of a readable text like HTTP 1.1 does, it allows for a far better compression ratio.

You can read more about the SPDY protocol at `https://www.chromium.org/spdy/spdy-protocol/spdy-protocol-draft3`.

On the other hand, we have the HTTP/2 protocol, which has been developed with the IEFT group and is in essence based on the SPDY/4 protocol. This will in the future replace SPDY on Google's platform.

The HTTP/2 protocol has the same characteristics as SPDY, and NetScaler supports both. Most web browsers today already support SPDY and HTTP/2, and the same goes for most web servers.

The way to enable SPDY and HTTP/2 is to create an HTML profile and bind it to a vServer. However, HTTP/2 is not supported on VPX and will therefore fall back to SPDY.

If a client connects to a vServer that has HTTP/2 and SPDY profile enabled, the communication will try in the following order:

- HTTP/2
- SPDY
- HTTP 1.1

The HTTP profiles can be found under **System | Profiles | HTTP Profiles**.

Here, we can make the change, as shown in the following screenshot, to enable HTTP/2 and SPDY. Choose ENABLED under the SPDY parameter. This will enable SPDY v2 and v3 and allow the client to negotiate between the two, then add the checkmark on HTTP/2, as shown in the following screenshot:

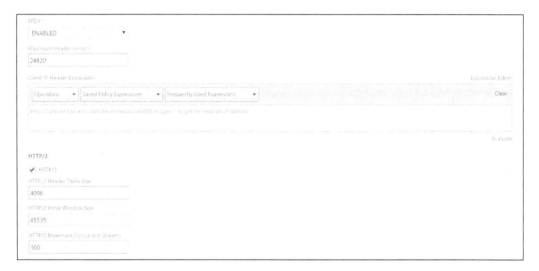

Summary

Throughout this chapter, we have gone through different features that can enhance network performance, both on the TCP level and on the HTTP level. We also discussed the different SSL parameters that should be adjusted in order to have the right level of security.

In the next chapter, we will take a closer look at the different high-availability features, such as GSLB, Failover, and Clustering, that are available in NetScaler.

6
High Availability

The purpose of many NetScaler instances is to provide load balancing and high availability for services. This should be the case for NetScaler itself as well; so, configuring it as a high-availability pair should always be considered. Sometimes a single HA setup might not be enough and we need to scale across multiple NetScalers or even multiple datacenters. These are some of the topics that we will cover in this chapter:

- Different scenarios for high availability
- Setting up high availability
- Redundant interface sets
- GSLB — the basics
- Clustering — the basics

Setting up high availability

Consider the scenario where we have a NetScaler sitting in front of our numerous services, and thousands of different websites that are load balanced and monitored by NetScaler.

So what will happen when NetScaler goes down, and the services stop and are no longer available for the end users? That's why we should always consider setting up a high availability NetScaler solution for our services.

By having a high availability NetScaler solution, we can ensure that if one of the appliances go down, we still have another one or more that is available to serve the requests and load balance the different services.

NetScaler has many solutions that we can use to ensure high availability. The most commonly used deployment is an active-passive pair. This means we have two appliances that cooperate so that one of the nodes is active (primary) and responds to requests and maintains the connectivity to the servers in the backend, and the other node sits passively (secondary) waiting to take over if the active node goes down.

By default, this feature uses GARP to broadcast its MAC address via layer two since both of the nodes use their own MAC address. When a device failover occurs, the secondary node sends out GARP packets to update the MAC table of nearby nodes (switches, routers, and firewalls) so that the new requests are sent to the new node. Also, NetScalers in an HA pair will also share SNIP addresses, meaning that the passive node will have the IP address listed, but it will be listed as passive. Therefore, to set up NetScaler in an HA pair, we only need one IP for SNIP and two NSIP addresses.

It is important to note that some firewalls do not support GARP, or GARP is blocked, and therefore, we need to configure VMAC for the deployment. When using VMAC, the MAC address is shared between the two nodes, and therefore, it is not required to use GARP to update the MAC table on nearby nodes. I'll come back to this later in the chapter and see how we can configure VMAC.

So, if the primary node were to go down or if it stops responding to requests, the secondary node will take over. The nodes monitor each other using heartbeats that are sent between the NSIP address of each of the nodes.

By default, there are some ports that need to be open in the firewall to allow for communication between the nodes in the high availability setup, as follows:

- The UDP port 3003 is used to exchange heartbeats for communicating UP or DOWN status
- The TCP port 3008 is used for secure high availability configuration synchronization
- The TCP port 3009 is used for secure command propagation and for the **Metric Exchange Protocol (MEP)**
- The TCP port 3010 is used for high availability configuration synchronization
- The TCP port 3011 is used for command propagation and for the MEP

High availability is included in every edition of NetScaler and supports a maximum of two nodes. It is important to note that this feature requires us to have two of the same models and the same main release build version. Running an HA pair with, for example, a MPX 5550 and a VPX 1000 is not supported by Citrix. However, even it is not supported, it will still work.

In order to set up a high availability pair from one of the nodes, we need to know the following information about the other node—the IP address and the default system username and password. It is also required that they have the same RPC passwords; by default, this is the same across NetScaler. To set up a high availability pair, go to **System | High Availability | Nodes** and click on **Add** from one of the nodes. Here, we are presented with the following options:

- **Remote IP address** (The NSIP of the other node)
- **Configure remote system to participate in high availability setup**
- **Turn off HA monitor on interfaces that are down**
- **Turn on INC (Independent Network Configuration)** on self node
- **Remote System credentials**

All we need to do is enter the IP address, configure the remote system to participate, turn off HA monitors on interfaces that are down, and enter a different username and password if it differs from the node we are configuring it on.

Turning off HA monitors on interfaces that are down means that NetScaler will not try to send HA probes from one node to another on interfaces that are not in use.

The last option is that INC is needed if the appliances are on different subnets and therefore require independent network configurations, since the regular HA option sets them up using the same network configuration.

After we have entered the information and clicked on **OK**, the primary node will start to propagate its information and configuration with the secondary node and set up a high availability pair.

It will also start to synchronize files such as SSL certificates and application firewall XML files; you can view the different files that are part of the synchronization process at `http://support.citrix.com/article/CTX138748`.

It is important to note that there are a few items that will not be synchronized, and these are licenses and `rc.conf` files.

Irrespective of whether the HA pair is active/passive, you will still need one active license of each of the nodes.

There might be issues with syncing SSL certificates; you can verify that they have been synced using the CLI command:

```
sync ha files ssl
```

Since it is set up in an HA pair, changes that are made to the primary node will be propagated to the secondary node. We cannot make changes from the secondary node, this is shown in the CLI and GUI.

We can view the configuration from the GUI or using the following command:

`Show ha node`

In CLI, it shows us which is the primary (active) node and which interfaces are active.

We can also use failover interface sets; if we have multiple network interfaces on NetScaler attached on different switches, we can use them to failover to another interface. This is covered later in the chapter.

In the GUI, we can right-click on each of the nodes and configure actions such as force sync and force failover. Force failover allows us to manually failover if, for example, we need to upgrade.

If we double-click on a node (the one we are logged into), we get a configuration screen where we can set how the HA pair should function.

By default, when the primary node goes down, the secondary node will take over and promote itself to primary. When the main primary node comes back online, it promotes itself again to the primary node. If we, for example, have a small upgrade process and the primary node goes down, the secondary will take over. If we do not want the secondary to promote itself during the upgrade process, we need to set the secondary node as **STAYSECONDARY**. This stops the process and the primary mode will remain as primary after the reboot.

In this menu, we can also define how often the nodes should send probes to monitor if the nodes are responding.

If you are having some issues with the HA feature, we can use the nsconmsg feature by using the CLI. By running the nsconmsg -d event command, we can get a live view of events that are happening directly in the console.

By default, NetScaler uses **Gratuitous ARP (GARP)** to advertise its MAC address after a failover has occurred. Some older firewalls from vendors such as Cisco and Juniper do not accept the type of GARP request packets that NetScaler sends out. So, if failover is not working in your environment, there is a slight change that needs to be made in order for GARP to function, by logging into the CLI of NetScaler and running the set network L2param -garpReply enabled command.

This command needs to be set on both of the nodes in a high availability setup.

If our firewalls or routers do not support GARP, we can configure NetScaler to use VMAC. VMAC allows NetScaler to have a floating MAC address between them, therefore bypassing the ARP problems with GARP. This can be configured by navigating to **System | Network | VMAC**.

Here we have to define a virtual router ID, for example 100, and bind it to an interface where the VIP requests come from. The virtual router ID is just used as an identifier within the VMAC. After this is done, the HA nodes will replicate addresses, and if we now go to **Network | Interfaces**, we can see a VMAC pane that shows the virtual MAC address, which both the appliances use.

If we set up a high-availability pair of NetScaler in, for instance, Azure or Amazon, we need a different approach since the NetScaler HA feature uses GARP or VMAC, which is not supported in these public clouds. I have written a quick comparison and description on how to set it up in Azure on my blog at `https://msandbu.wordpress.com/2015/05/22/when-to-use-traffic-manager-cloud-service-load-balancing-or-citrix-NetScaler/`.

For Amazon, I suggest heading over to the deployment guide from Citrix at `https://www.citrix.com/content/dam/citrix/en_us/documents/products-solutions/deployment-practices-and-guidelines-for-netscaler-amazon-web-services.pdf`.

Setting up high availability across different subnets

If we want to achieve high availability across different subnets, we need to alter some configurations on the HA pair. For instance, if we have another NetScaler appliance in a different subnet, it might require a different route table or even other NAT rules in place in order to communicate with the backend resources. In a traditional HA setup, all the different static/dynamic routes are synchronized across the HA pair, and they also share the same SNIP address.

In order to make this work, we need to configure **Independent Network Configuration** under the **HA** settings. This can be done using the command:

```
Add ha node id IPAddress -inc ENABLED
```

Using this command, the NetScaler, by default, does not propagate settings that are unique to that particular network, such as:

- IPs (NSIP, MIP, and SNIP)
- VLANs

- Routes
- Dynamic Routing
- Reverse NAT

This allows us to have a unique configuration for each node in the HA pair. It is important to note that the VIP is floating between the HA-pair; therefore, even if the nodes are located across different subnets, the NetScalers still needs a way to publish the VIP address publically.

Redundant Interface Sets

Redundant Interface Sets is a feature that allows us to have multiple interfaces connected but only one interface is active and the others are in standby mode. This enabled us to, for instance, have redundant network connections to different switches on, in case we want to have redundant NIC settings on NetScaler.

Unlike, for instance, LACP, where we need to configure the NetScaler and the peer device, this feature requires no configuration on the peer device. The only thing that the peer device needs to support is GARP broadcasts.

In case redundant interface sets are configured, only the active interface will accept traffic; the standby interface will drop any receiving traffic and will not send out any packets.

In case an active interface goes down, the second interface, which is based on a priority will broadcast a GARP containing its MAC address and where it is located, and will resume the traffic that was dropped from the primary interface.

Some important things to note. In an HA-setup, redundant interface sets will not be propagated across or get synchronized with the other node. These settings are locally unique.

Also, this feature is not supported in a clustered environment because of the architecture, and we should use LACP as an alternative.

In order to create a link redundant set, we need to navigate to **System | Network | Channels**, then click on **Add**. Under **Channel ID**, choose **LR** from the list, the **LA** option is for link aggregation.

Leave the **MAC** value as blank; the NetScaler will then generate a custom MAC address for the purpose. This MAC address will be used across all the different interfaces.

Then we need to add the interfaces that are a part of the set, then it should appear as shown in the following screenshot:

Alternatively, you can use the following CLI command:

`Show channel`

In the command line, we can see which interface is the primary adapter. In case of multiple interfaces, we might want to configure a specific priority on the different interfaces so we know which interface will be the secondary adapter, the third adapter, and so on.

This can be configured by navigating to **System | Network | Interfaces** for each interface that is a part of LR. We have a new option called LR priority. The one with the lowest priority will always become the primary adapter in a set.

Clustering

Now, besides the regular high availability feature that requires the use of two nodes, NetScaler also has some other high availability features such as clustering.

We will not dive deep into clustering, but we will be going through a basic overview. If you wish to read more about clustering, you should read the clustering guide from Citrix, which can be found at `http://bit.ly/1NLPPIA`.

Regular high availability operates with a two-node instance, where one is active and the other is passive. With clustering, we can scale from 2 up to 32 nodes, which are operating in an Active/Active state. This allows for a large amount of traffic throughput. In order to use this, we require an additional license. Also, there are some other requirements, as follows:

- To be on the same subnet
- To be of the same hardware type (for example, physical appliances)
- To be of the same platform type
- To have the same licenses (Standard, Enterprise, and Platinum)
- To be of the same software version and build
- To have their own feature license to be able to use clustering

Here, we can configure all NetScaler nodes from a single IP called the cluster IP, which in essence replaces the NSIP for management, so they act as one logical entity. The cluster IP is owned by the configuration coordinator, which is in essence the cluster coordinator role, which floats between the different nodes within a cluster.

Every VIP address that we create will automatically be available on all the nodes (called striped IP address) in a cluster; every **Subnet IP (SNIP)** address can also be distributed to all the nodes (striped IP address) or be available from just one node (spotted IP address). Citrix recommends using striped IP addresses for SNIPs.

Clustering can be set up either using **Equal Cost Multiple Path (ECMP)** or using cluster link aggregation.

ECMP is a routing protocol; it defines that a route has multiple paths to the destination with the same cost. This means that if I have multiple roads that I can travel to get to a destination and the distance is equally far, I just choose one of the paths. This way we can distribute traffic between the paths.

Different network vendors have different mechanisms to handle ECMP traffic. For example, Juniper uses a hash algorithm to determine if a packet should travel one path or another. Citrix has written an article on how to configure this using a Cisco Nexus 7000, which is available at `http://support.citrix.com/proddocs/topic/ns-system-10-map/ns-cluster-traf-dist-ecmp-tsk.html`.

Cluster link aggregation is an extension of link aggregation, which means we have one interface connected from all the nodes to a switch to create a virtual interface. So, instead of a regular link aggregation where we have multiple interfaces from the same appliance, we have one interface from many appliances.

 It is important to note that not all features running on a clustered environment are supported, for example, NetScaler Gateway. A list of supported services running on a clustered deployment can be viewed at `http://support.citrix.com/proddocs/topic/ns-system-10-5-map/ns-cluster-feat-supp-ref.html`.

Global Server Load Balancing

Now we also have **Global Server Load Balancing (GSLB)**. This is not a high availability feature per say; however, as the name describes, it is a load balancing feature.

GSLB works with the help of DNS. It allows us to deliver a service from different data centers spread across different geographical locations; this helps us in case of data center failures and disaster recovery.

It can also help to spread the load across different locations with its proximity feature, and allows users to be sent to the closest data center. This type of feature is already in use today is many large web services such as Google, Facebook and so on.

So, let's take a closer look at how GSLB works. First off, it is important to know how DNS functions, as this is the fundamental component in GSLB.

When a user connects to a service, for example, `www.myservice.company.com`, the client will send a DNS request to its DNS server, which is the NS server. The DNS server of the client will send a recursive request to the authoritative DNS server of that record. The authoritative DNS server will respond with an A-record to the recursive DNS server, which will in turn respond to the client.

Now, the client and the recursive DNS server will store the A-record in their cache based upon the **time-to-live** (TTL) entry of the record. When the TTL expires, the client has to once again query the DNS server. This is the component that allows GSLB to work, as GSLB in essence is load balancing and DNS. For example, with GSLB configured and the client again querying for the service `www.myservice.company.com`, the DNS server has a list of different A-records for that particular service that might represent a list of vServers on an HA-pair NetScaler on a site. This can also depend on the setup, which might return with an A-record for the closest vServer that is able to handle the request.

Now, there are different ways to configure DNS with GSLB here, which are as follows:

- **Authoritative DNS configuration**: This allows NetScaler to act as an authoritative DNS server for a domain, in this case, `company.com`. This means NetScaler will respond to all DNS queries from a recursive DNS server, and based upon where the client is located, respond with an A-record that is closest to the `client.g`.

- **Authoritative sub-domain DNS**: This allows NetScaler to act as an authoritative DNS server for a subdomain, for example, `myservice.company.com`.

- **Proxy DNS vServer**: This allows NetScaler to proxy DNS requests to an authoritative DNS server running inside the corporate network. NetScaler has a vServer DNS service running, which load balances DNS queries externally to an internal or another external DNS server.

There are also some key concepts we need to be aware of before setting up GSLB:

- **GSLB Site:** This is typically a datacenter or a specific region. For instance, if we have a datacenter in New York and London, this will be created as two sites in GSLB.

- **GSLB Service:** This is typically a load balanced vServer in each site. So, for instance, if we have an HTTP load-balanced vServer in each of the locations, we will have two GSLB services, HTTP 1 for London and HTTP 1 for New York.

- **GSLB vServer:** This is a GSLB service that is then represented by one or more GSLB services. So, here it would be represented by the two HTTP servers from each GSLB site.

- **Domain Name:** This is the FQDN that represents the particular GSLB vServer. In this case, the domain name will be contoso.com.

- **Authoritative DNS Server:** This is the Nameserver that is responsible for the name lookup for the domain contoso.com.

So, in this case, we could have one of the NetScalers configured as an authoritative DNS server. This can be done by adding a particular service on NetScaler called ADNS.

This can be done using the following command:

```
add service Service-ADNS-1 10.14.39.21 ADNS 53
```

After we have added an ADNS server, we can start to create the sites. First, we create the London site and choose type LOCAL. This is done by navigating to **Traffic Management | GSLB | Sites**. Here, we also need to choose a site IP address. NetScaler uses this IP to communicate with other GSLB sites. After this is done, we need to enter a new site that represents the other datacenter, just change the type to Remote and enter the site IP for that GSLB site.

After we are done with this, we need to do exactly the same configuration on the other site. The only difference is that we change the type and add the first site we created as the remote site. This is important because, by default, GSLB does not propagate setup like HA, and therefore they are not aware of the setup on the other site.

Then, we need to add the different GSLB service that will be included in the GSLB setup. Go to **GSLB | Services** and then click on **Add**. Here, we have the option to choose the site name and whether the service is a new server or already represented as a virtual load balanced server on NetScaler, as shown in the following screenshot:

After that, we need to add the other services, which are represented on the other site as well. Except that we just change the site location. We also need to run this setup on the other site as well.

After we are done adding the services, it is time to create a GSLB virtual server. This is located under the **GSLB** pane | **Virtual Server** and then click on **Add**. Enter a name, choose **A** as the record type if the service is using IPv4, or AAAA if it is using IPv6, then click on **OK**. This will give us a bunch of different configuration options.

The only necessary option we need to configure is GSLB virtual server to GSLB service binding.

Here, we configure the different services that make up the virtual server, for example, Domains.

Here we enter the FQDN of the GSLB virtual server.

If we now view the zone name locally on the NetScaler by navigating to **Traffic Management | DNS | Records | Address Records**, we can now see GSLB FQDN listed as a record entry. In order to verify that DNS is working properly, we can specify the aDNS service as our DNS server and use the following command:

```
Nslookup GSLBDOMAINNAME
```

This should return one of the services that is attached to the GSLB virtual server.

In a real-world scenario, we will need to contact our domain registrar to update the NS records for a particular zone, then we will need to have a public IP for our ADNS service. This will allow external users to be able to do DNS queries against it and be load balanced.

If you want to learn more about GSLB, we have an upcoming book called Mastering NetScaler VPX, which will be available later this year that has a larger section dedicated to GSLB.

It is important to note that GSLB is an advanced feature and can be configured with many different load balancing options, such as:

- Active/Standby
- Active/Active
- Proximity
- Weighted round robin
- Data center persistence

It is also important to understand how DNS works in order to troubleshoot properly.

Summary

Now that we have explored some of the different high availability features that NetScaler offers, it is also important to keep in mind that running NetScaler in a virtual environment requires planning with regards to where to place it. It is also important to have some sort of availability feature in place for the virtualization hosts, as having a high availability feature on NetScaler is not enough if something happens to the virtualization hosts.

We can consider having the following features:

- **Failover cluster**: This allows us to have redundant virtualization hosts in case of hardware failure and so on
- **NIC teaming**: This ensures continuous availability in case of NIC failure
- **Raid on local disks**: This ensures that the system continues to run in case of hard drive failures
- **SAN redundancy**: This ensures that the storage on which NetScaler resides is redundant

And, of course, these features should always be used in combination with a redundancy in NetScaler, as in regular high availability, for instance.

Security and Troubleshooting

NetScaler often sits in front of large web services processing large amounts of data. Some of these services may contain credit card transactions or may serve sensitive data. It is therefore crucial that NetScaler is properly configured to protect such data. Also, with such a large amount of data going through the application, we may be required to troubleshoot network traffic or a session in general.

The following are some of the topics that we will go through in this chapter:

* Protecting services in NetScaler
* Protecting services using AppFirewall
* AppFlow and integration with NetScaler Insight
* Traffic analysis and Wireshark

Protecting services in NetScaler

Now, since NetScaler often sits in front of many different services, this may make it a popular target for hackers. These might, for instance, be PCI-DSS services, such as VISA or PayPal. On the other hand, they may just be plain web services that might be an intranet portal or some other sort of sensitive data.

So, the purpose is to configure NetScaler to deflect common forms of attack and activate counter measures when someone is trying a particular form of attack.

A popular question that is often asked is, should NetScaler be in front of the firewall or should the firewall be the first line of defense?

In my opinion, NetScaler has sufficient security features to allow it to be placed in front of the firewall. Putting it behind the firewall often makes the network more complex and makes it more difficult to handle VMAC, GARP updates, and so on.

NetScaler has many prebuilt defense mechanisms, for instance, **Denial of Service (DoS)** attacks on the TCP layer. The default TCP profile `nstcp_default_profile` has a setting called TCP SYN Cookie, which in essence stops DDoS attacking using TCP SYN Flood.

Under TCP Profiles, we also have the option to enable SYN Spoof Protection. This feature is not enabled by default, but it can help NetScaler to stop attacks coming from spoofed SYN packets.

We have some similar capabilities under HTTP profiles. In the default `nshttp_default_profile` we can, for instance, enable Drop invalid HTTP requests, which helps against HTTP attacks if the requests do not follow the appropriate standard.

HTTP DoS protection

In some cases, it might not be that easy to detect an attack. For instance, in a suspected HTTP DDoS attack, a web server may be attacked with legitimate traffic, and therefore they are regular HTTP requests. This is where we can use HTTP DoS protection. HTTP DoS protection allows NetScaler to respond with a JavaScript challenge to all incoming HTTP requests. Now, since an HTTP DDoS attack is typically done using a cluster of multiple nodes running a scripted attack, these nodes do not support any form of JavaScript request. Therefore, when they cannot respond to the JavaScript challenge, NetScaler closes the connection. Regular users who surf through a regular browser that supports JavaScript are therefore granted access. This happens in the background, and the user never sees that it happens. Enabling HTTP DoS puts a lot of strain on NetScaler, especially if there is a lot of traffic and the client detect rate is at 100 percent.

To enable HTTP DoS, navigate to **Security | Protection | HTTP DoS**, and click on **Add**.

Then, provide the policy with a name and enter a queue depth—a representation of the number of outstanding requests to the system—before the HTTP DoS feature is enabled. Next, enter a client detect rate: this is a percentage value between 0 and 100 that defines the percentage of requests that should get the JavaScript challenge after the HTTP DoS feature is triggered. By default, the value is set to 1% in the global HTTP DoS parameters.

After we have created an HTTP DoS policy, we must bind it to our services. Go to **Traffic Management | Services**, then choose the services that this should be enabled for. Next, go into policies and click on the + sign and choose HTTP DoS, where you will find the newly created policy.

It is also important that we define thresholds on the NetScaler services. If not, NetScaler will not know how many requests or clients the backend services can handle, and the HTTP DoS feature will never be triggered.

These values can be set under **Services | Thresholds**.

Access lists

NetScaler also has support for the traditional **access control list** (**ACL**), where we can define four types of lists. All of them have the option to define protocol, but simple ACLs only support TCP/UDP, while extended has a long list of different protocols, such as EGP, ICMP, GRE, and so on.

- **Simple ACL**: This defines only DENY rules for source IP addresses.
- **Simple ACL6**: This defines only DENY rules for source IPv6 addresses.
- **Extended ACL**: This allows us to define DENY/ALLOW/BRIDGE rules for source IP, source-range and destination IP, or destination IP-range. It also allows us to configure source MAC and destination MAC.
- **Extended ACL6**: This allows us to define DENY/ALLOW/BRIDGE rules for source IPv6, source-range and destination IPv6, or destination IPv6-range. It also allows us to configure source MAC and destination MAC.

Simple ACLs are only stored in memory and cannot be seen in the running configuration, so when we define a simple ACL, it has the TTL of 8 seconds and therefore expires and gets deleted. Simple ACLs are memory-effective and should therefore only be used to block out single IP addresses for a period of time.

Extended ACLs do not have an expiration timer, and they give granular control over when we want to ALLOW/DENY traffic.

An example of extended ACL in the CLI might look like this:

```
add ns acl ext_block_bad_ip ALLOW -srcIP = 100.0.0.0-101.0.0.255
-protocol TCP -priority 10
```

By default, an ACL is not active. This can be seen by running a show ACL and seeing the effective status on it. In order to apply an ACL, we need to append the following parameter to the end of the command:

```
-kernelstate APPLIED
```

It is, however, important to remember that the packet processing that takes place on NetScaler will run the packets through any eventual simple ACLs first before they are evaluated against the extended ACLs.

Protecting services using NetScaler AppFirewall™

NetScaler is equipped with many security features that can fend off attacks, which we have talked about earlier in this chapter. These features include:

- SYN DoS Protection
- ACL
- HTTP DoS

These are just some of the features that can be used, but most of these features only look at the connection or further down the ISO layer, and not so much on what kind of content is in there. In today's IT environment, the most common form of attack occurs using SQL injections, HTTP brute forcing, CSRP attacks, and so on. This is where the application firewall comes in.

The application firewall is used to secure services running behind NetScaler. It consists of policies and profiles. Here, we use the policy to identify patterns in the traffic. Profiles — like most features in NetScaler — are used to specify what we are going to do with the traffic.

The application firewall delivers protection in two ways. The first is signature-based. This means that NetScaler recognizes a pattern based on a signature and, depending on the action, may drop the connection. So this method is useful if it is a known vulnerability that a hacker is trying to exploit.

The second way the application firewall can offer protection is with deep protection features that are used for unknown attacks. Here we can configure it with a learning feature. This learning feature can be a useful way to see, for example, which websites the users are allowed to access internally and which they are not. This allows NetScaler to adapt a standard behavior.

We can also define filters in deep protection features. For example, users are allowed to access a website but not a URL starting with /mysite or /sales, and we can define an action when someone tries to access a URL with /mysite.

Thus, deep protection is useful for URL masking, SQL injections, buffer overflows, managing forms, and so on.

 It is important to note that application firewall is only part of NetScaler Platinum and can be purchased as an add-on in Enterprise. It is also recommended that you update the signature file when a new version is released. If your NetScaler is allowed to communicate externally using NSIP, it is also possible to configure auto update. This can be done by navigating to **Signatures** | **Action** | **Auto Update Settings** and enabling **Signatures Auto Update**. After this is enabled, go to **Action** and trigger the update version.

Now that we have talked a little bit about how application firewall works, let us go deeper and see how it operates. However, we cannot go through every feature within the application firewall, since it contains so much advanced functionality. We are only going to go through the basic features and some of the deep protection features. If you are interested in knowing more about the features not covered in this book, I suggest you head over to the eDocs article available at `https://docs.citrix.com/en-us/netscaler/11/security/application-firewall/security-checks-overview.html`; it contains information about all the different deep protection features.

Before we start using the application firewall feature, it must be enabled. This can be done by using the GUI under **System** | **Settings** | **Basic Features** | **Application Firewall** or by using the following CLI command:

```
Enable ns feature appfw
```

Then, go to **Security** | **Application Firewall** and start configuring the features. To see how to enable the different protection features, go through **Application Firewall Wizard**.

This will start a wizard where we first need to define the name of a web application. This is not linked to vServers but is used just for descriptive purposes. We also need to define a web application type that defines what choices we get in protection features. So as an example, let us say that we want to secure a regular IIS site running on Windows Server 2012, which is basic HTML. Then we can enter the name `IIS` and choose regular web application **HTML** under **Type**.

Next, under **Rule**, define a rule that allows NetScaler to identify what traffic it should look at. Here we can use many of the same expressions we use on the other features, and we can also type in `true`. Then this rule will apply for every connection made to NetScaler. If we want application firewall to only protect a certain site, we must define a rule expression, for instance, based on the hostname of the site: `HTTP.REQ.HOSTNAME.CONTAINS("ecommerce")`.

Next, define signatures that we want to enable for this particular site. So, choose **Create New Signature** and then click on the **Simple Edit** mode and click on **Continue**. This will list different categories of built-in signatures, as shown in the following screenshot:

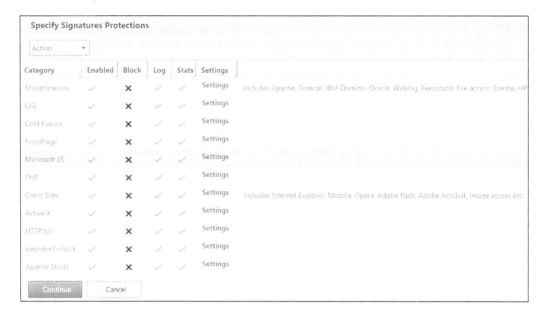

As we can see, by default these categories are enabled, but they will never block any traffic. What they will do is just log anyone that has, for instance, triggered an attack within these signatures. If we, for example, were setting up an application firewall rule for an IIS site, we could activate block for all Microsoft IIS rules by right-clicking on Microsoft IIS and choosing **Enable Block** for this category.

Now, in order to see what all the different signature files for IIS do, navigate to **Signatures | Default Signatures** and choose **Edit**. From there, filter the view based on `web-iis`, following which of the 100+ rules should appear. From there choose a rule and click on **Edit**. Here we can see the particular pattern match that the signature looks for, as in the following screenshot:

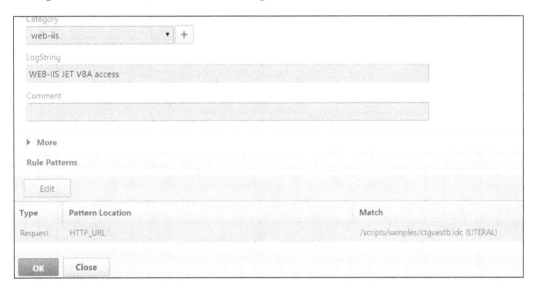

After we have defined which signatures are to be part of the web application protection, we can continue with the deep protection feature.

Remember that these features are enabled to deal with an unknown attack, so we can use the learning feature to define a baseline or go in and change the default behavior. This feature applies for XSS, SQL injections, and more, but for now let's just leave it at the defaults, as shown in the following screenshot, where we can take a closer look at some of the protection features:

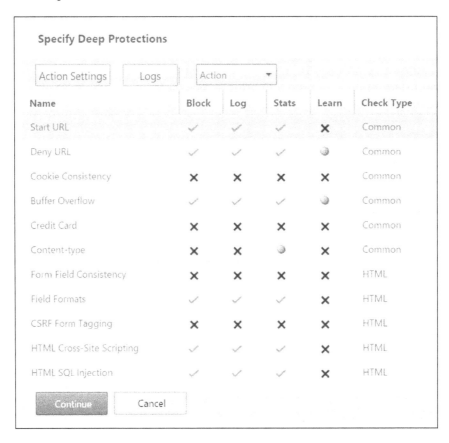

Name	Block	Log	Stats	Learn	Check Type
Start URL	✓	✓	✓	✗	Common
Deny URL	✓	✓	✓	◐	Common
Cookie Consistency	✗	✗	✗	✗	Common
Buffer Overflow	✓	✓	✓	◐	Common
Credit Card	✗	✗	✗	✗	Common
Content-type	✗	✗	◐	✗	Common
Form Field Consistency	✗	✗	✗	✗	HTML
Field Formats	✓	✓	✓	✗	HTML
CSRF Form Tagging	✗	✗	✗	✗	HTML
HTML Cross-Site Scripting	✓	✓	✓	✗	HTML
HTML SQL Injection	✓	✓	✓	✗	HTML

The **Start URL** action defines which URL a client is allowed to use to start a connection against a service. This means that the first connection from our client can go directly to `http://mycompany.com/index.html` but not directly to `http://mycompany.com/employee/me`.

This function is used to prevent forceful browsing, which means preventing repeated attempts at random URLs. So URLs entered here cannot be used with, for example, bookmarks, since they are direct URLs.

By default, the feature is set with the following values:

- **Log**: NetScaler will log the violations made
- **Stat**: This will maintain the statistics for the rule
- **Block**: NetScaler will block all URLs that do not match the rule

We can also enable **Learn**, this enables NetScaler to learn what the default start URLs made to a website are, which makes it easier to deploy rules based on what the most accessed start URL is. NetScaler will then eventually mark that URL as the Start URL and users will then be able to only use that URL to access the start page.

But for now, we can click on **Continue** and **OK** to finish the wizard setup. If we go back to **Application Firewall | Profiles**, we can continue with the customization of the different deep protection features.

If we click on **Edit** on our newly created profile, we are presented with security checks. Here we see deep protection features that are active for our profile and what values are set for each feature. We also have a pane called **Relaxation Rules**, where we can define different parameters for each deep protection feature. For instance, if we go into **Start URL** under **Relaxation Rules** and click on **Edit**.

If we do not have the learning feature enabled, we need to predefine a start URL here. If we want all our users to start on `index.html`, we can add this by choosing **Add** and entering the URL.

These features use regex to search through the URLs to see if they violate a rule. Regex uses a sequence of characters to form a search pattern. Using these features within NetScaler requires a bit of knowledge about them. Fortunately, NetScaler includes a regex tester that allows us to test our expressions. This can be accessed within a feature by going to **Profile | Open Start URL | Add | Regex Editor**. If you are unsure how an expression should look, you can find a good list of examples at `https://docs.citrix.com/en-us/netscaler/11/security/application-firewall/url-protections/starturl-check.html`.

However, we can enable the blocking action and leave the rest at its default, and make sure that the **Learn** action is enabled.

If we go back to **Deep Actions** under **Relaxation Rules**, we also have the **Deny URL** action. This is basically an allow/deny action. If we click open, we get a list of URLs where we can define the users that are not allowed to browse, as shown in the following screenshot:

Now, here we can add different URLs that the users are not allowed to browse. We can also define different regex queries to not allow users to directly access scripts, such as this query:

```
http://www[.]example[.]com/((([0-9A-Za-z]|\\x[0-9A-Fa-f][0-9A-Fa-
f])\n([0-9A-Za-z_-]|\\x[0-9A-Fa-f][0-9A-Fa-f])*/)*([0-9A-Za-z]|\\x[0-
9A-Fa-f][0-9A-Fa-f])\n([0-9A-Za-z_-]|\\x[0-9A-Fa-f][0-9A-Fa-f])*[.]
(bat|js|sql)$
```

Now, by default, this policy will be bound at a global level, meaning that it will apply to every service on NetScaler. If we want to bind it to a specific service, we should unbind it at a global level and bind it to a specific service.

 It is important to note that using application firewall on a global level will put a lot of strain on NetScaler, since it has to analyze every HTTP packet.

Now, to change the bindings, go to **Application Firewall | Policy Manager | Default Global**. Here you can see that the application profile you created is now bound there. Choose **Unbind** and then run the Policy Manager again, and this time choose the load balancing vServer or the content switching vServer that you wish to bind the profile to.

If we now start to do some random requests against the web service, we can see that the statistics start to fill up. These can be viewed by navigating to **Application Firewall | Statistics**. Here we can see that the different security checks will have their own statistics pane.

Now, let's deploy some rules for the deep protection features. First, we can define for deny URL that we can disallow access to the /admin /setup URL. Go into **Application Firewall | Profiles**, choose the newly created profile, and click on **Edit**. From here, go into **Security Checks** and choose **Deny URL**, then mark the **Block** action. Next, go into the **Relaxation Rules**, choose **Deny URL**, and click on **Edit**. Then, enter the different URLs to deny access.

Every user who tries to access a random URL on the service that triggers a violation rule will automatically get redirected to the main page. We can define a custom redirect URL for those who try to access random URLs or a custom HTML page

This can be done by navigating to **Profile**, then click on the newly created profile and choose **Edit | Profile Settings**, and then under **HTML settings**, define either a **Redirect URL** or **HTML Error Object**. When a user now tries to log in to the URL of the vServer with an /admin or /setup, they will be redirected to the custom error object.

Now, since we also specified that the start URL feature should use the learning capability, we can see what it has learned from the different web requests. This can be seen by going into the **Application Firewall Profile**, choosing **Edit**, and going into **Learned Rules**. From here, choose the **Start URL** and click on **Edit**.

Here we can view a list of URLs that have been learned and those that have been accessed. We can, from here, click on a rule and choose **Deploy**, which will take the URL and make it the **Start URL**, as shown in the following screenshot:

Under **Learned Rules**, we also have an option called **Trusted Learning Clients**, which allows us to restrict the learning module to only apply to a certain number of IP addresses. After we have defined a start URL, we only need to apply the **Block** option under **Security Checks** and then click on **Apply**. So when a user opens a new connection to the vServer, the start URL must match the one we defined. If not, the user's request is violated and will therefore be sent to the redirect page or the HTML custom error page.

We have now seen a small portion of what application firewall has to offer; it offers a wide range of different features that can be used to prevent Cross Side Scripting, SQL injections, and so on. As mentioned earlier, if you wish to learn more about the different features within application firewall, head over to this eDocs article at `https://docs.citrix.com/en-us/netscaler/11/security/application-firewall.html`.

Using AppFlow® to monitor traffic with NetScaler Insight Center™

Now, in most cases, NetScaler is used as a central component to deliver high-availability services to users, both internally and externally. This means that NetScaler, in most cases, handles a large amount of traffic.

What happens if a user complains about the slow performance of an application, or that something is running sluggishly? Or if we want to get an overview of the number of users accessing our services? This is where AppFlow comes in.

AppFlow is a feature in NetScaler that is used to collect web performance data and database information. It can also be used to gather performance from ICA sessions. It is built on the IPFIX format, which is an open standard defined in RFC 5101.

Take a look at the following screenshot, for example:

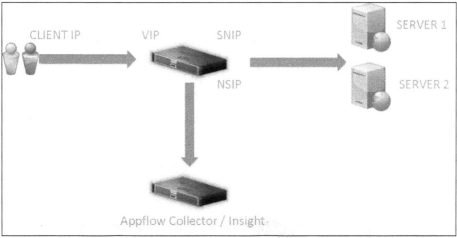

When a client opens a connection to the VIP of NetScaler, it will perform a new connection to the backend server, and then the traffic will be returned from the backend server back to NetScaler and then to the client. The AppFlow feature will send data to a collector with information about the client that connected. The information includes which port and service it accessed and which backend server it got connected to. So we have the complete overview of all the conversations that a client has with a service.

By default, NetScaler uses its NSIP to deliver data to an AppFlow collector. It is important to note that we can use net profiles to define AppFlow to use another IP address, for instance, an SNIP.

Viewing AppFlow data requires that we have a collector that is capable of analyzing the data. We can, for example, use other third-party AppFlow connectors such as SolarWinds or Splunk that have the capabilities to analyze AppFlow data. Citrix also has a solution called NetScaler Insight, which acts as an AppFlow collector. NetScaler Insight is a virtual appliance that runs either on XenServer or VMware. This appliance can be used as a collector for AppFlow, which allows us to get an overview of the Web and ICA traffic.

NetScaler Insight 11 has an option to scale out the deployment using three different components:

- **Agents**: These are used to communicate with the different NetScaler and CloudBridge appliances and will then forward AppFlow logs to the connectors. These agents are also only used for HTTP-based traffic flows.

- **Connectors**: The connectors receive AppFlow data from the different agents, which are then evenly between the different backend database servers.

- **Database**: The database node receives and stores the data coming from the different connectors.

We can select which role we want when deploying the Insight virtual appliance, as shown in the following screenshot, which displays the CLI options after the first boot:

```
NetScaler Insight Deployment Type. This menu allow you to set an
ent type.
Selecting the listed number allows deployment type selected.
--------------------------------------------------------------------
     1. NetScaler Insight Server.
     2. Connector Node.
     3. Database Node.
     4. NetScaler Insight Agent.
     5. Cancel and quit.

Select a choice from 1 to 5 [5]: 1
```

There is also a built-in sizing guide on Insight. In the main dashboard, go into **Configuration | NetScaler Insight Center | Insight Deployment Management**, and enter the necessary requirements. It is important to remember that the first server must be selected as a NetScaler Insight Server.

When setting up NetScaler Insight either on XenServer or VMware, just import the OVF file, and it will automatically create a VM with the required configuration. The Insight appliance also runs on FreeBSD. FreeBSD is an open source operating system that is built on Unix.

Remember to put the Insight appliance on a network where it can reach the NSIP of NetScaler.

The start configuration of Insight is required to be done from CLI. We need to enter an IP address and a subnet mask to allow us to communicate with it using the GUI.

After we have entered the required IP configuration, we can access it by opening a web browser against the IP address. The username and password is the same as the NetScaler appliance, that is, nsroot and nsroot.

The first time we log in, we are presented with a dashboard with two main panes: **Dashboard** and **Configuration**. In order to get AppFlow traffic, we need to add a NetScaler instance. The first time we log in, we are presented with a dashboard which allows us to enter the information of either a NetScaler or a CloudBridge instance, as shown in the following screenshot:

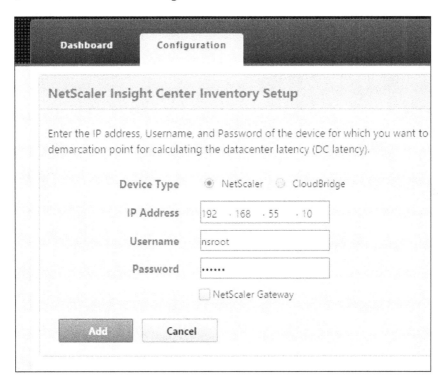

After we have added an appliance, it will show us a list of vServers for which we can configure AppFlow. For example, if we have a load balanced vServer we wish to be able to see AppFlow data for, we can right-click on an LB server and choose **Enable AppFlow**.

Now we are presented with a policy window where we need to enter an expression. If we wish to get AppFlow data for all traffic that goes to the vServer, we can use the following expression:

```
HTTP.REQ.LB_VSERVER.NAME.EQ("nameofvserver")
```

This will create an AppFlow policy and bind it to the vServer on the NetScaler appliance. We can also enable this for a Content Switching vServer and a NetScaler Gateway vServer.

In order to enable AppFlow for a NetScaler Gateway vServer, right-click on vServer, choose Enable **AppFlow**, and insert `true` under expression. This will allow NetScaler to generate AppFlow data for Gateway vServers as well.

> In the latest release of NetScaler Insight, we can now integrate it with the Google geo-coding API in order to get geo-information about clients who are connecting to our vServers. This requires a GeoLite database which can be downloaded from `http://geolite.maxmind.com/download/geoip/database/GeoLiteCity.dat.gz`.

We have now configured NetScaler Insight against NetScaler. When new clients connect to a vServer that has an AppFlow policy bound to it, data will appear in NetScaler Insight.

When we go into the dashboard, we are presented with two options: **Web Insight** and **HDX Insight**.

> It is important to note that the amount of data that the Insight appliance stores depends on what kind of license the NetScaler appliances are running. If we have the NetScaler Standard license and we wish to use it with Insight, we can only use the Web Insight functionality. If we have NetScaler Enterprise, we can use Web Insight, but the HDX Insight data will only show traffic for the last month. If we have NetScaler Platinum, we can use Web Insight, and HDX Insight will be able to show traffic for the last year.

Web Insight shows us AppFlow data that is generated from load-balanced vServers and Content Switching vServers, and shows us information regarding the Web traffic. HDX Insight shows us the data generated from the NetScaler Gateway vServer.

For example, if we go into Web Insight, we can browse to different categories that show us which clients have access to a server. This is shown in the following screenshot:

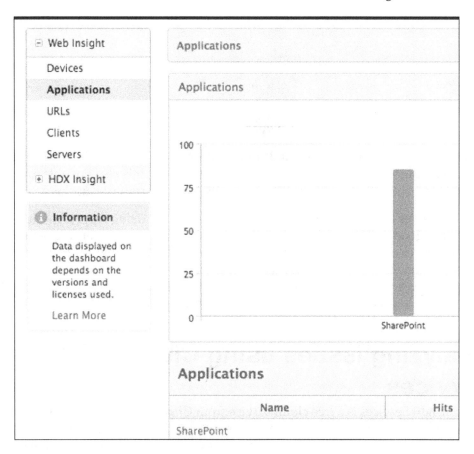

And if we go into HDX Insight, we can get an overview of how many users are accessing our gateway and what applications they are accessing.

We will also get other key information, such as:

- **WAN latency**: This is the average latency caused by the client-side network
- **DC latency**: This is the average latency caused by the server network
- **ICA RTT**: This is the average screen lag that the user experiences while interacting with an application or desktop hosted on XenApp or XenDesktop
- **Bandwidth**: This is the rate at which data is transferred over the ICA session

These can be seen in the following screenshot:

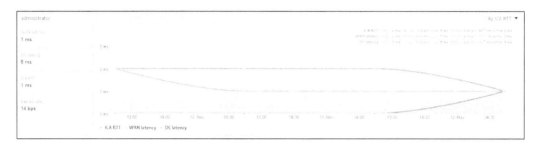

We have now successfully set up and configured AppFlow integration with NetScaler Insight. If we have a XenDesktop environment, it is also possible to integrate Insight with Director to get a live view from the traffic usage here.

Now, this gives us a look at the network flow of services. Using AppFlow with Insight is a good feature to use to get an overview of how many users are actually using the services and what content they are accessing. But AppFlow does not give us the information we need in case we want to troubleshoot something, for example, if a user has issues connecting, the network is getting sluggish, or a service is marked as down and we need to dig a bit deeper to find the issue.

Analyzing issues using Citrix Insight Services

Citrix Insight Services is a free cloud service from Citrix that allows us to upload detailed logging information and configuration from our NetScaler and scan it against a set of rules to see if there are any issues or best practices that we have not configured. It is also often used in conjunction with Citrix support cases, and Citrix will often tell you to upload data to Insight Services before it can continue troubleshooting.

In order to generate log files for Citrix Insight Services, we need to go into **System | Diagnostics**, and then from there click on **Generate Support File**, or use the following command:

```
Show techsupport
```

This will generate a `tar.gz` file under the folder `/var/tmp/support/collector_ip_data.tar.gz`, which can be downloaded to a local machine using, for instance, winSCP or any other FTP-based client.

You can also enable a feature called **Call Home**, which will allow NetScaler to automatically upload a tech support `tar.gz` to insight services in case of a critical error or failure. This can be done using the following CLI command:

```
Set callhome -emailaddress email@domain.com
```

After we have downloaded the `tar.gz` file, we need to upload it to Insight Services. Go to `https://taas.citrix.com/AutoSupport/`.

From here, we need to login with our Citrix account, then we need to choose **Upload data**.

When we choose **Upload data**, we have the option of entering a case number, in case we have a support case with Citrix for troubleshooting. But in our case, just click on **Upload Data**.

Then it will take a couple of minutes to do the analysis. For larger instances, it might take more time. TaaS will notify you with an email to your contact address, which is listed with the Citrix account after it is done with the analysis.

Now, when the analysis is done, it can go through the running configuration and give us some feedback regarding best practices on our instance, as shown in the following screenshot:

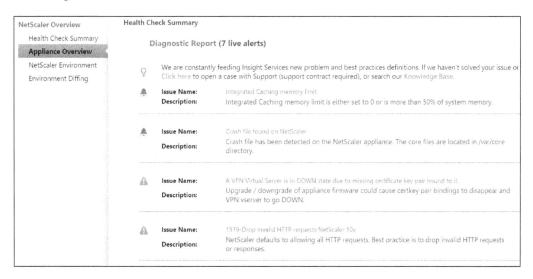

We can also do a drilldown on each of the different alerts to get more detailed information about a state, and even get command line examples on how we can fix the issues. We can also get a detailed overview of the performance on NetScaler, on CPU, packets, memory, and so on.

Traffic analysis with NetScaler® tools and Wireshark

There are times when you need to get your hands dirty to troubleshoot something in a detailed sense to find out what is actually wrong. For example, why you are having trouble with NetScaler, why a client is having trouble connecting, or why the network is not working as it should.

NetScaler has a number of built-in tools that we can use to gather information for basic troubleshooting. For example, we have the regular tools such as `ping` and `traceroute` to verify network connectivity. We also have commands as follows:

`show connectiontable`

This allows us to show connections in real time, which also can be used in conjunction with `grep` to make it easier to see if a particular client has a correct connection with NetScaler, for instance:

`Show connectiontable | grep -I "192.168.0.50" | grep -I "HTTP"`

This will only display connections that are from 192.168.0.50 and are running over the HTTP protocol. We can also use the show command for other features as well, such as ICA. We can use it to show if users are connected to an ICA session using the following command:

`Show vpn ica connection`

`Show vpn stats`

We also have some kernel commands such as `dmesg` which will display all system message logs since the last reboot. For instance, if you are having IP conflicts or a lot of ARP-based traffic, it will be displayed there.

Also, NetScaler has a long list of different log files located under `/var/nslog` where it stores different content, such as the `newnslog` files.

We can use the command `nsconmsg` to report events in real time, as well as to parse through statistical data. For instance, if we want to view old `newslog` files, which NetScaler archives by default every two days in order to view statistical data on our load balanced vServers, we can use this command:

`nsconmsg -K /var/nslog/newnslog -d oldconmsg -s ConLb=2`

This will run through the newslog. The `-d` operator is to display performance data and the `-s ConLb=2` parameter is for the level of load balancing events to display. The capital `K` means that it is in read mode; typing a small `k` means write, which means that we might overwrite our log files.

We can also combine this with, for instance, `grep` and `pipe` to filter out what we need. Now, we also have other tools which we can use to perform more detailed network analysis, such as:

- `nstrace`
- `nstcpdump`

Both of these tools are accessible from the GUI by navigating to **System |
Diagnostics | Start new trace** and using the CLI.

The difference between these tools is that `nstrace` dumps packets in the native NetScaler format; this has an advantage since it has information regarding clients connecting to a VIP. It connects from SNIP to a backend server. It will also list proprietary header information such as VLAN, NIC, and PE details.

> It is important to note that a trace file generated with `nstrace` can also be analyzed with Wireshark, but this requires a modified version of Wireshark that has NetScaler filters installed. At the time of writing this book, the current development build supports NetScaler 11.
>
> `Nstcpdump` does not give the native NetScaler trace format. It is more resource-intensive, but it gives an ordinary `tcpdump` trace file that we can analyze in, for example, Wireshark.

So by using `nstrace` we can, for example, get trace files for one of our vServers. This requires the use of specific filters. If we do not use filters here, we will get all of the network traffic in the trace file, which, again, can be analyzed using Wireshark filters.

For instance, to get a trace file for our vServer called `vpx` using `nstrace` from CLI, we could use the following filter:

```
nstrace.sh -filter "vsvrname == vpx"
```

Or if we wanted a trace file for our backend service called `IIS`, we could use the following filter:

```
nstrace.sh -filter "svcname == IIS"
```

We could also filter based upon IP addresses or port numbers, as follows:

```
nstrace.sh -filter "sourceport >= 80 && destip != 88.88.88.88"
```

You can press *Ctrl + C* to terminate the trace using the CLI.

These are just some examples. To get a list of all the different filter abilities, you can use the `help nstrace` command. You can also use `nstcpdump` for more low-level troubleshooting. In order to use it, enter the shell mode under CLI. This can be done by typing `shell` when in the CLI. With `nstcpdump`, you can also use filters, but not specific to any NetScaler resources.

For example, `nstcpdump` can be used to create a trace file for all traffic going via `port 80`, as follows:

`nstcpdump.sh port 80`

Or, it can be used to filter, for example, all traffic from a specific host using TCP, as follows:

`nstcpdump.sh dst host 10.0.0.20 and tcp`

We also need to specify a location for the trace files, or else they will all appear in the console. This can be done by appending the `-w` option and defining a path, as follows:

`Nstcpdump.sh dst host 10.0..0.2 -w /var/nstrace/filename.cap`

When using GUI, we can also append filters directly to add a trace without knowing the parameters that we need to use. Using the **Start new trace** option, we have the option to start and stop a trace and then download the trace files directly to our computer. By default, all trace files are stored under `/var/nstrace/date`. It is important to note that debugging a trace requires some sort of protocol analyzer to sort the data, this is where Wireshark comes in.

Wireshark is an open source network protocol analyzer. We can use it to monitor live time on a network interface or use it to analyze trace files. It is very powerful and the most commonly used one for troubleshooting network issues where we have a trace file.

So let's go through a basic troubleshooting scenario just to show how you would have troubleshot network issues in real life. This scenario will cover how you can start a trace file using `nstcpdump`, download it, and then import it to Wireshark.

We can also use a bunch of different filters to sort the data, which I will cover a bit. By default, Wireshark just lists all the packets sorted by package ID.

Wireshark can be downloaded from `http://www.wireshark.org/` and runs on the most common operating systems. Another tool that is also useful in this type of scenario is Microsoft Message Analyzer. The advantage of using Microsoft Message Analyzer will be evident when you need to troubleshoot Microsoft-specific services, such as SMB traffic. You can download Message Analyzer from `http://www.microsoft.com/en-us/download/details.aspx?id=40308`.

Let us go ahead with an example scenario, just to show how we can use Wireshark to analyze and debug traffic. In this scenario, a user has recently tried to access a vServer called IIS, which is a basic load-balanced web server running Windows Server 2012 R2 with the IP address `192.168.88.100`. The user tries to connect with a web browser but the connection times out. The client is located on `192.168.88.1`. Let us see if we can find out why.

We can start the trace using `nstcpdump` in the GUI. Remember to put the packet size to 1514 if we want the entire packet, which in some cases makes it easier to see the entire conversation, although it puts more strain on NetScaler and creates a larger trace file. Also, remember that when using HTTP compression on that particular vServer, create a policy for that particular IP and exclude it from compression. Since compression *encrypts* the information using compression algorithms, it makes it a bit harder to troubleshoot.

After this is done, we ask the user to try connecting again. We gather some packets and then we can stop the trace and download it from the GUI.

After we have downloaded the trace file to our computer, we can open Wireshark and from there go to **File | Open**, and then choose the trace file. Immediately, this will list all the packets from the trace file, sorted by packet ID, as shown in the following screenshot:

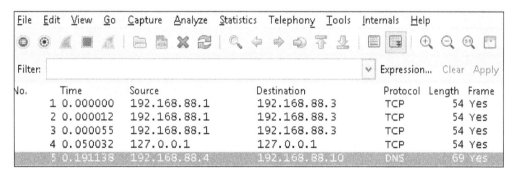

So all packets are listed with a source, destination, protocol, length of the frame, and more information on what is inside the packet. If it is a regular HTTP protocol packet, we can see the information that has gone back and forth in clear text.

We also have a filter box where we can enter different filters to the trace file. A good overview of the use of different filters in Wireshark can be found at `http://wiki.wireshark.org/DisplayFilters`.

In our example, we can use the following line in the filter box and then choose **Apply**, since we know that the client is connecting from that IP address:

```
Ip.src == 192.168.88.1
```

This will now update the window with all packets coming from that IP address, and it still contains all of the different protocols. To narrow it down to HTTP, we can add the following line of code:

```
Ip.src == 192.168.88.1 and http
```

This leaves us with three packets left to analyze. From here, we can see that the client did an HTTP GET method against the main URL with a PNG and an ICO file on the website. **GET** is the **HTTP** method that is used to request content from a server, as shown in the following screenshot:

No.	Time	Source	Destination	Protocol	Length	Frame	Info
532	29.281545	192.168.88.1	192.168.88.20	HTTP	332	Yes	GET / HTTP/1.1
549	29.324924	192.168.88.1	192.168.88.20	HTTP	387	Yes	GET /iis-85.png HTTP/1.1
968	29.437566	192.168.88.1	192.168.88.20	HTTP	275	Yes	GET /favicon.ico HTTP/1.1

So, we can see that the client did request the content. What we can do next is look at the TCP packets that are linked to this request. Right-clicking on one of the packets gives us an option called **Follow TCP stream**. This is useful since it shows us the entire conversation that the client and our web server had, and we are presented with stream content. This shows what was requested and what was returned from the web server in clear text.

This is useful because it allows us to see what HTTP data is being sent and what is being returned to the client. It is also useful when we are working with configuring caching and compression.

So from the TCP stream, we can see all the information that was presented to the client—not just HTTP data, but all the other data that is attached to the resource. For example, from the trace file, we can get Wireshark to export objects inside it.

By going to **File** | **Export Objects** | **HTML**, we will get a list of objects that are referenced in the HTML traffic. For example, we can export the image files that are part of the trace file.

Analyzing encrypted content with Wireshark

When we look at the TCP stream, we see the conversation the client had with the vServer and that the vServer responded correctly with the content, as shown in the following screenshot:

```
Follow TCP Stream                                    –  ☐   ✕
Stream Content
GET / HTTP/1.1
Accept: text/html, application/xhtml+xml, */*
Accept-Language: nb,en-US;q=0.8,en-GB;q=0.5,en;q=0.3
User-Agent: Mozilla/5.0 (Windows NT 6.3; WOW64; Trident/7.0; rv:11.0) like Gecko
Accept-Encoding: gzip, deflate
Host: 192.168.88.20
Connection: Keep-Alive

HTTP/1.1 200 OK
Age: 1
Date: Mon, 10 Feb 2014 07:54:43 GMT
Connection: Keep-Alive
Via: NS-CACHE-10.0:   2
ETag: "63311bc03a1bcf1:0"
Content-Type: text/html
Last-Modified: Mon, 27 Jan 2014 08:35:36 GMT
Accept-Ranges: bytes
Server: Microsoft-IIS/8.5
Content-Length: 701
```

So, it is only safe to assume that the client received the content and there is most likely something wrong with the client setup.

Since the trace file is in pure HTTP traffic, it means that it is in clear text, which makes it easy for us to make the trace file and see the entire conversation between the client and the server. But in most cases, when we have a load-balanced web server, it runs HTTPS, so the entire conversation is encrypted.

So, if we generate a trace file for the HTTPS service, we are unable to read what is specifically happening at the HTTP layer. All we can see is below the HTTP layer, for example, that an IP address has connected to another IP address using HTTPS and port nr.

The following is a screenshot of the TCP stream from a conversation between a client and a server using HTTPS:

```
Follow TCP Stream                                ↔    –  ☐   ✕
Stream Content
.............R....`.o...1.....+T...>c.R..y.6. ...P.,....1.......D.5(..3.g..fK...$.+./.....
...9.5.........3.2...../.
...k.........ad.msandbu.local......
.................#..3t......". .spdy/2.spdy/3.spdy/3.1.http/1.1uo...............^...z..
R...
... j..o...Iaj....|./8..(.E ...P.,....1.......D.5
(..3.g..fK............3t...http/1.1.......... .k.....nL%@.G...G\p|.9aY*.
(...@o..........DI..JyV.1..v...A}'!...+..9y...,...x......W
...)[=
```

With Wireshark, we can actually decrypt HTTPS packets in the trace files as long as we have the private key from the digital certificate that was used on the vServer.

You would only need to download the private key from NetScaler if you have created a certificate from scratch; it can be easily downloaded from NetScaler by navigating to **Traffic Management** | **SSL** | **Manage Certificates** | **Keys** | **CSRs**. If you have a PFX file, you need to use OpenSSL to export the private key from it. OpenSSL can also be found under the **SSL** pane. From there, run the following command:

```
openssl.exe pkcs12 -in publicAndprivate.pfx -nocerts -out
privateKey.pem
```

This can also be started from the CLI. So, after we get a hold of the private key, we need to add it to Wireshark. In Wireshark, go to **Edit** | **Preferences** | **Protocols** | **SSL**. There, under the RSA keys list, choose **Edit**. Then from there choose **New**. Now, enter the IP address of the vServer, which appears in the trace files we want to decrypt. Also, we need to enter the port nr, which is 443, and the protocol, which is http. Then, point it to the private key that has been downloaded from NetScaler.

Next, click on **Apply**. Wireshark will then update the trace logs with the decrypted data. And we can now once again use filters to locate the particular conversation between the client and the vServer.

As we can see, Wireshark is really useful in debugging network traffic from a trace file. We have only touched the surface of what we can do with Wireshark; it is also beneficial to have a firm understanding of networking if we are to do troubleshooting with Wireshark.

Citrix has some posts regarding how to best use Wireshark to debug Citrix connection issues, which can be found at http://support.citrix.com/article/ ctx121696 and http://support.citrix.com/article/CTX138202.

Summary

In this chapter, we went through some of the different ways that we can configure high availability on NetScaler, and we saw how to analyze traffic using Wireshark and nstrace.

Also, we went through AppFlow with NetScaler Insight to get a glimpse of how much traffic is entering our network. And lastly, how we can protect our service using application firewall. In the next chapter, we will go through the different features of the AAA module.

8
AAA Application Traffic

NetScaler is often used as a secure gateway solution to publish Citrix applications such as XenApp or XenDesktop, or it can also be used to proxy connections to backend services such as SharePoint or Exchange. Also, we can use NetScaler as an authentication point to securely publish resources that we want to protect behind a two-factor authentication mechanism, or we can use it to restrict access to different internal resources that are all part of the AAA module. In this chapter, we will cover the following topics:

- What is AAA?
- Configuring AAA for a virtual server
- Authorization and security levels
- Other resources

AAA is a term that stands for **authentication**, **authorization**, and **auditing**. This contains many different subfeatures of NetScaler. An important thing to remember is that this feature is only a part of the enterprise and platinum license of NetScaler.

Let's look closely at an example to see what we can do with this feature. For instance, we want to publish an internal web application that, by default, does not have any form for authentication. We want to securely publish this application externally and only then have it be available to the users who are authenticated against LDAP. We want to restrict some specific part of the web application to the external users, and we want to have logging in place to make sure that we can audit the authentication attempts. This can be done with the AAA feature by creating a load balanced virtual server representing the web service. Then we can create a AAA virtual server with an LDAP policy attached to this. Now we can bind the AAA virtual server to the load balanced virtual server. After this, we can create an authorization policy that restricts some URLs. These are then bound to the load balanced virtual server. Finally, we will create an audit policy, which is then attached to the AAA virtual server to log all the authentication attempts.

From an end user's perspective, the logon process will look like this:

1. User 1 sends an HTTP GET request to `test.no/hr.pdf`, which is a load balanced vServer on NetScaler.

2. NetScaler receives the HTTP requests on the vServer, but sees that the virtual server has an authentication server bound to it and tries to match it against a session cookie on the client side. If the session cookie is not found, the user is redirected to the AAA vServer.

3. User 1 is redirected to the AAA vServer, which has an LDAP policy attached to it. The user is presented with a username and password login page.

4. User 1 enters his AD username and password in the logon page.

5. The AAA vServer tries to authenticate the username and password against the domain controller and sends a log to the audit policy server.

6. The AAA vServer gets an acknowledgement from the AD controller and sends an Auth OK back to the client.

7. User 1 client session is then redirected back to the load balanced vServer. This time it contains the session cookie and ID. The HR AAA group has an authorization policy enabled that defines that if a user belongs to the HR group, they are allowed access to the content:

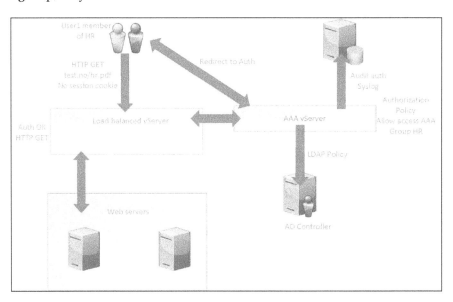

So, in order to set up this we first need to enable the AAA feature, which can be done using the following CLI command:

```
Enable ns feature AAA
```

The AAA feature can also be enabled by right-clicking on **AAA | Application Traffic** under the **Security** pane and choosing **Enable**. Now, before we start creating an AAA vServer we should configure a particular global setting first. This can be done under **AAA | Change Global Settings**.

As a best practice, we should configure the default authorization rule to DENY, and use authorization policies to allow access to those that we want to give access.

Setting up an AAA vServer

Now we can create an AAA vServer to which the users are redirected. Go to the **AAA | Application Traffic** pane and click on **Virtual Servers** and click on **Add**.

Here under the settings we need to enter a name, IP address, and port number. By default, it is set to SSL and 443. Also, we have an optional parameter, which is the Authentication domain. Here we need to enter the FQDN of the AAA vServer if we want to use Forms-based authentication.

Forms-based authentication is an authentication mechanism that is wrapped around a combined HTTP and HTML code, where a user enters their user information in web forms and clicks on **Submit**.

If we click on the **More** button we will have some additional parameters, which are important to think about:

- Failed login timeouts
- Maximum login attempts

These define the number of times a user can try to authenticate against a vServer, and how long the user will be locked out if they have tried too many times. By default, these values are not set and should be configured in order to reduce the number of attacks, such as a dictionary attack or a brute force attack.

After we are done entering the values, we can click on **Continue**, and we will be prompted to enter a server certificate and a CA certificate. These need to be added before the virtual server becomes active.

After we have added both the certificates, we can start defining authentication policies. These policies define how NetScaler should authenticate users who try to access it. For instance, if this is based on LDAP, RADIUS, SAML, and so on, then this is defined by an expression that NetScaler needs to evaluate when receiving the connection.

Authentication policy

Let's start by creating a basic authentication policy using LDAP, which will allow our users to log in using their Active Directory credentials when they are redirected to the AAA vServer. First click on the **+** sign and choose **LDAP** as **Primary Type**.

In the **Expression** pane, type `ns_true`. This means that all the traffic that enters this vServer will have this policy. Then click on the **+** sign on the server and enter the information in the Active Directory server.

After we are done adding an LDAP server and finished with the LDAP policy, we can go to **Authentication | Dashboard** to see the status of our LDAP servers:

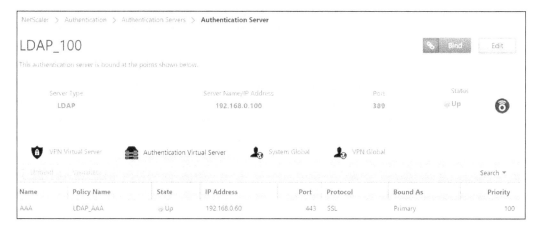

From the preceding screenshot, we can see that the server is responding to LDAP and that it is bound to a particular AAA vServer.

Now that we are done creating an AAA vServer and adding a basic LDAP authentication policy, we need to bind it to a service on which we want to have authentication.

An AAA vServer can either be bound to a Content Switching vServer or a Load balanced vServer. In this example, we have a load balanced vServer.

Go in the **vServer | Edit | Choose Authentication** pane on the right-hand side.

Now we have two options to choose from, **Form Based Authentication** or **401 Based Authentication**. A form based authentication will present a Citrix-based login page that allows users to enter the username and password in HTML forms. This will then be authenticated against the LDAP policy we have. This type of authentication will create a session ID that will be stored in the client browser. A 401 based authentication uses HTTP to present a dialog box on the browser where we will enter our username and password.

 A 401 based authentication is the same as Basic Authentication in IIS.

For now, we are going to use a forms-based authentication. Since this presents a web page, we need to enter the FQDN of the AAA vServer, as NetScaler will redirect users to that particular vServer.

Then choose an authentication virtual server type and set this to **Authentication Virtual Server**, and then choose the AAA vServer in the drop-down menu below. Also, we have an alternative option called **Authentication Profile**, but this is covered a bit later in this chapter.

Now the configuration should look as follows for the load balanced vServer:

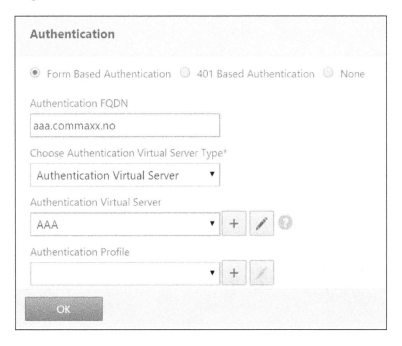

Click on **OK** and then **Done**.

If we now try to browse the FQDN of the load balanced vServer, we should be presented with a Citrix login webpage. After logging in with an LDAP-based credential, we will be forwarded to the load balanced servers.

> NOTE: If we are having issues authenticating against an LDAP server, we can check the status for our authentication attempts under **Authentication** | **Logs**, or we can use the command line to debug using the following:
>
> ```
> Shell
> cd /tmp
> cat aaad.deug
> ```
>
> Another place to check for authentication attempts is on the security log on the particular LDAP/AD server.

Authorization policy

Now that we are done with a basic authentication policy, we can add an authorization policy that defines whether a client/user is allowed or denied access to a resource.

We can bind authorization policies to any of the following:

- AAA user
- AAA groups
- Load balanced vServer
- Content Switching vServer

For this example, let's start with a policy that we will bind to the same load balanced vServer and then create a new authorization policy that we will bind to a particular AAA user.

Go to **Security** | **AAA Application Traffic** | **Policies** | **Authorization**, then click on **Add**. Now, let's say that we want to allow users to have access to a particular range of IP addresses. We can start by giving the policy a name and choosing the action ALLOW. In the **Expression** field, type CLIENT.IP.SRC. BETWEEN(192.168.0.0,192.168.0.5).

After we are done, we will click on **OK**. Now we need to bind the authorization rule to a vServer. Go to the same load balanced vServer that we used earlier for AAA authentication and click on the **Policies** pane. Click on the **+** sign and choose **Add Authorization Policy** and choose the one we have just created.

Now, we try to open up a web browser and again go to the FQDN of the load balanced vserver. If we have a client computer that resides within that IP address range, we will be allowed access to the resource after we are authenticated. It is important to note that authorization policies are processed after authentication policies. This is because we might have authorization rules that are attached to a AAA user or group, which can only be processed after a user has been authenticated.

Now, let's say that we want to allow access to a particular AAA user, even though they are outside of that IP-range. What we first need to do is create an AAA user; this can be done under **AAA | Users**, from here click on **Add**. Then, enter the username of the LDAP user and click on **OK**.

Now we have four options that we can bind to this user:

- AAA groups
- Authorization policies
- Session policies
- Audit policies

We will start by adding an authorization policy directly to that user. Click on the authorization policy pane and create a new policy. Choose the **ALLOW** action, and in the **Expression** field type ns_true. This is done because we want this particular user to have access, since the default authorization rule is deny.

We can also define more granular-based access. For instance, if we wish to deny access to PDF files that are accessed via our load balanced vServer.

To do this, we create a new authorization policy, set action to deny, and enter the expression, HTTP.REQ.URL.SUFFIX.EQ("pdf").

After we are done creating the policy, we need to bind it to the vServer. If, for instance, we have a user who is allowed access via an authorization policy, the user will still not be able to access the PDF files, since the strictest rules always win.

However, this policy will only trigger when the URL suffix is PDF, so the user will still be able to open other files types on the same service.

Authentication profiles

Now by default, we can use the same AAA vServer and attach it to many different vServers. When a user is authenticated for one of these resources, the user is also given access to the other resources, since he has already been authenticated. In some cases, we might need to define different security levels for our services. For instance, if we require a two-factor authentication to access some services, or we just want another level of authentication in order to access the service.

This can be done using authentication profiles. Within an authentication profile, we can define what level of access a user is given after they are authenticated. We can also define to which domain the user is given access.

Authentication profiles can be created by going to **AAA | Authentication Profile** and then clicking on **Add**.

From here, we need to enter a name for the profile, FQDN of the AAA vServer, choose the AAA vServer we want to redirect authentication to, and then we need to enter the important bits, namely, authentication domain and authentication level.

These are both optional settings but can provide better security for published services. For instance, if I have an authentication profile with an authentication domain and when a user authenticates, the browser will get a session cookie with the domain name set. Therefore, if I have other resources that I publish using the same domain, the user is automatically allowed in. If I set up resources using another domain, the user will need to be re-authenticated. The authentication level also provides greater security. For instance, if we have an authentication profile with the security level set to two, users who are authenticated are only allowed to access the resources that have the same security level or lower. This means that if a user tries to access a resource that is below the security level of one, they would need to be re-authenticated. So let's follow this with an example.

We have two web services that we want to publish with external authentication. One of the services is accessible to all users and will therefore be given a security level of five. The other service is only available to users who are authenticated using the two-factor authentication, and therefore will be given a security level of one.

First, we need to two load balanced vServers in place that will present the two web-services. Next, we need to create two authentication profiles. In order to make this example simple, we will be using the sample AAA vServer. The best approach will be to have two AAA vServers, where one of them has a simple LDAP policy bound and the other has LDAP and RADIUS for two-factor authentication.

So, we can start by creating a simple authentication profile for all external users, which should look like the following screenshot:

Then we will create the other authentication profile that looks the same, except that we change the security level to one and change the profile name.

After we are done creating both the profiles, we need to bind them to the load balanced vServers.

Now, while binding them to the vServer, it is important that we choose authentication profile instead of authentication vServer, since the AAA vServer is already referenced in the profile.

We will bind the one with the highest security level number (5) to the vServer for all users, and we will bind the other with the lowest number (1) to the other service where we want better security.

You will notice now that if we try to authenticate first to the vServer that has the authentication profile for all external users, we will be granted access. If we try to change the URL to the other vServer, we will be given a new login page again, since we do not have the right amount of security level.

Troubleshooting AAA and setting up audit policies

In some cases, it might be necessary to troubleshoot if an AAA policy is not correctly configured or some users are having issues accessing certain services. This might be challenging as well because of a mix of many authentication and authorization policies and a combination of users and different groups.

So, where can we start to troubleshoot?

First, the AAA feature has a monitor that allows us to see active user sessions. This can be viewed under **AAA | Active User Sessions**. It can list all the users who currently have an active session against NetScaler using the AAA module, or even using ICA. In this view, we can see whether a user has been successfully authenticated and if they are able to access a service.

If a user is not able to authenticate, we might need to start the `aaad.debug` feature within CLI to be able to pinpoint the authentication process. Another possibility might be that we can run a trace during the authentication process. If we are using a regular LDAP-based authentication, we can see the LDAP traffic using, for instance, Wireshark.

Another option might be to look inside the security log in the particular domain controller that is being used for authentication.

Another good idea is to check whether the user has an active account in the domain. This can be checked from any computer that is a part of the domain using the following command:

```
Net user /domain username
```

We can also enable AAA-enhanced authentication feedback that will give the user details about what the issue might be if they are having issues authenticating.

This can only be set on a global level and is applicable for both AAA-TM sessions and NetScaler Gateway sessions. It can be activated using this CLI command:

```
Set aaa param -enableEnhancedAuthFeedBack
```

The AAA-enhanced authentication feedback can also be activated using the GUI by navigating to **NetScaler Gateway | Global Settings | Change authentication AAA settings** and enabling it from here.

When a user tries to log on and fails, the user can get one of the following error codes:

- `4001`: Invalid credentials. Catch-all error from previous versions
- `4002`: Login not permitted. Catch-all error from previous versions
- `4003`: Server timeout
- `4004`: System error
- `4005`: Socket error talking to authentication server
- `4006`: Bad (format) user passed to nsaaad
- `4007`: Bad (format) password passed to nsaaad
- `4008`: Password mismatch (when entering new password)
- `4009`: User not found
- `4010`: Restricted login hours
- `4011`: Account disabled
- `4012`: Password expired
- `4013`: No dial-in permission (RADIUS specific)
- `4014`: Error changing password
- `4015`: Account locked

Audit policies

We can also enable auditing to keep a record of all authentication attempts, changes that are done, informational events, and so on of our services. NetScaler can either log to a Syslog server or it can store this, for instance locally on the appliance using a built-in Nslog server. Now, by default, when using NetScaler as an audit logging server, the `ns.log` file is rotated (new file is created) when the file size reaches 100K and the last 25 copies of the `ns.log` are archived and compressed with `gzip`.

In order to set up audit events, we first need to create an Nslog or Syslog server, where we define about what we want to get logging information and from what kind of logging levels we want.

 If we do not have a Syslog server available in our environment, we can, for instance, set up NetScaler Insight, which has the same capabilities. Also we can, for instance, use Solarwinds Kiwi Syslog or Splunk. It is important to note that Syslog uses UDP to transfer files, while Nslog uses TCP.

In order to set up an audit server, we can go to **System | Auditing** then choose either **Nslog** or **Syslog**, click on **Servers** and choose **Add**. If we want to use NetScaler locally to store log files, we will just enter 127.0.0.1 as an IP address and leave it as the default port.

We have some additional options to log TCP messages and ACL logging as well. Also, we can specify what kind of events should be logged, for instance, informational events or critical events.

After we have created an audit server, we need to create a policy. This, in essence, is to give the policy a name and bind it to an audit server. After this is done we can bind the audit policy to an object. For instance, if we want to bind an audit policy globally, we will go to **System | Auditing**, choose either **Nslog** or **Syslog**, click on the **Action** button, and choose **Global Bindings**. From here, choose the policy that we want to be bound globally, then click on **Bind**. Depending on the logging level, start creating log files under the /var/log folder on NetScaler. It is important that if you are storing the logs locally, there should be some sort of automated task that copies out the logs to an external location for audit purposes.

 We can bind an audit policy to an authentication virtual server, a user account, or to a group as well.

After we have bound an audit policy to an object, we can directly view the audit messages created on NetScaler using the Recent audit message or the Syslog viewer, which are available using the GUI and can be found under the **Auditing | Audit Messages** pane.

For instance, as shown in the following screenshot, within the Syslog viewer we have an ability to filter based on module, which makes it a lot easier to see the events related to the UI or the AAA module:

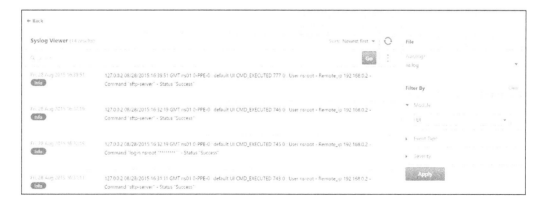

Summary

We have taken a closer look at how we can use AAA to enable authentication for our services, which are services of NetScaler. Also, we have taken a closer look at how we can use authorization rules to specify which content our users are able to access and which content they are not able to access. This chapter only gives a brief introduction to the AAA module. However, this module is capable of doing so much more. For instance, it can serve as an SAML SP, which can be used in conjunction with Active Directory Federation Services. Also, it can do SSO on behalf of the user to backend web resources.

 NetScaler AAA can act as an SAML identity provider as well, which in essence allows us to use it as a replacement for Active Directory Federation Services. This can be used, for instance, when we need to merge with Azure Active Directory or Office365. Citrix has created a guide for how you can set up NetScaler as an SAML iDP at http://support.citrix.com/article/CTX200818.

Throughout this book, we have just scratched the surface of what NetScaler can do. If you are interested in learning more about the different features of NetScaler or just want more information, I suggest that you head over to the following websites:

- My blog: http://msandbu.wordpress.com
- Citrix Blogs: http://blogs.citrix.com/
- NetScaler Rocks: http://NetScalerrocks.com

If you wish to reach out to me for any type of feedback regarding the book, or have any type of questions, do not hesitate to contact me on msandbu@gmail.com.

Thanks for reading!

Index

P

parameters, content group
  reference link 105
persistency groups
  about 92
  creating 92
persistency types
  reference link 74
platform license, NetScaler
  reference link, for downloading 7
Prefetch 108
Product Documentation, Citrix
  URL 82
public NTP server
  reference link 18

R

redirect URL 76
Redundant Interface Sets 130, 131
regular generic load-balanced service 68

S

SafeNet
  URL 37
sample expressions, Citrix
  reference link 38
SDX 4
Select Acknowledgement (SACK) 116
services
  protecting, in NetScaler 139, 140
  protecting, NetScaler AppFirewall™
    used 142-150
  weights, assigning to 75
setup scenarios, NetScaler 8
SharePoint 2013
  load balancing 83
simple ACL 141
simple ACL6 141
SmartAccess
  about 30
  reference link 30
SNIP 24, 25
SPDY
  about 121
  URL 121

SSL
  tuning 119, 120
SSL capabilities
  reference link 120
SSL VPN 30
statistics 76
StoreFront
  load balancing 78, 79
  reference link 78
StoreFront integration 46-49
Subnet IP (SNIP) 132
subnets
  high availability, setting up across 129
supported services, running on
    clustered deployment
  reference link 133
synchronization process
  reference link 127

T

TCP
  tuning 115-117
TCP customization, on NetScaler
  URL 118
TCP, options
  Forward Acknowledgement (FACK) 116
  Nagles Algorithm 117
  Select Acknowledgement (SACK) 116
  Window Scaling 116
TCP port 3008 126
TCP port 3009 126
TCP port 3010 126
TCP port 3011 126
testing 65
TFTP
  reference link 82
TFTP for provisioning servers
  load balancing 82
time-to-live (TTL) 134
traffic
  analyzing, with NetScaler tools 158-162
  analyzing, with Wireshark 158-162
tuning
  about 61
  GUI customization 64
  profiles 62, 63
  redirection 61, 62

U

UDP, for ICA proxy
  reference link 34
UDP port 3003 126
Unified Gateway 58-61
Use Subnet IP (USNIP) 24

V

version 11, NetScaler OS
  reference link 7
virtual environments
  tuning for 113-115
virtual load balancing server,
      DNS options
  Bypass AAAA requests 91
  DNS64 91
  Recursion Available 91
virtual private cloud (VPC)
  about 14
  reference link 14
virtual server (vServer) 33
VPN
  about 30
  deploying 50-53
VPX 5
VPX Express 6

W

web interface
  load balancing 79
Web Interface monitoring
  reference link 80
weights
  assigning, to service 75
Window Scaling 116
Wireshark
  URL, for downloading 160
  used, for analyzing encrypted
      content 163, 164
  used, for analyzing traffic 158-162
Wireshark, for debugging Citrix
      connection issues
  reference link 164

X

XML Broker
  load balancing 80

Thank you for buying

Implementing NetScaler VPX™
Second Edition

About Packt Publishing

Packt, pronounced 'packed', published its first book, *Mastering phpMyAdmin for Effective MySQL Management*, in April 2004, and subsequently continued to specialize in publishing highly focused books on specific technologies and solutions.

Our books and publications share the experiences of your fellow IT professionals in adapting and customizing today's systems, applications, and frameworks. Our solution-based books give you the knowledge and power to customize the software and technologies you're using to get the job done. Packt books are more specific and less general than the IT books you have seen in the past. Our unique business model allows us to bring you more focused information, giving you more of what you need to know, and less of what you don't.

Packt is a modern yet unique publishing company that focuses on producing quality, cutting-edge books for communities of developers, administrators, and newbies alike. For more information, please visit our website at www.packtpub.com.

About Packt Enterprise

In 2010, Packt launched two new brands, Packt Enterprise and Packt Open Source, in order to continue its focus on specialization. This book is part of the Packt Enterprise brand, home to books published on enterprise software – software created by major vendors, including (but not limited to) IBM, Microsoft, and Oracle, often for use in other corporations. Its titles will offer information relevant to a range of users of this software, including administrators, developers, architects, and end users.

Writing for Packt

We welcome all inquiries from people who are interested in authoring. Book proposals should be sent to author@packtpub.com. If your book idea is still at an early stage and you would like to discuss it first before writing a formal book proposal, then please contact us; one of our commissioning editors will get in touch with you.

We're not just looking for published authors; if you have strong technical skills but no writing experience, our experienced editors can help you develop a writing career, or simply get some additional reward for your expertise.

Mastering Citrix® XenDesktop®

ISBN: 978-1-78439-397-7   Paperback: 484 pages

Design and implement a high performance and efficient virtual desktop infrastructure using Citrix® XenDesktop®

1. Design, deploy, configure, optimize, troubleshoot, and maintain XenDesktop for enterprise environments and to meet emerging high-end business requirements.

2. Configure Citrix XenDesktop to deliver a rich virtual desktop experience to end users.

3. A comprehensive, practical guide to monitoring a XenDesktop environment and automating XenDesktop tasks using PowerShell.

Citrix XenApp® 7.5 Desktop Virtualization Solutions

ISBN: 978-1-84968-968-7   Paperback: 328 pages

Plan, design, optimize, and implement your XenApp® solution to mobilize your business

1. Optimize your XenApp solution for the best end user experience.

2. Design a robust infrastructure for application and desktop delivery.

3. Easy to follow guide that will help you to utilize the capabilities of the Citrix XenApp environment.

Please check **www.PacktPub.com** for information on our titles

Citrix® XenMobile™ Mobile Device Management

ISBN: 978-1-78217-214-7   Paperback: 112 pages

Gain an insight into the industry's best and most secure Enterprise Mobility Management solution

1. Deploy and manage the complete XenMobile solution.

2. Learn how to customize and troubleshoot your XenMobile apps.

3. Step-by-step instructions with relevant screenshots for better understanding.

Getting Started with Citrix XenApp 6.5

ISBN: 978-1-84968-666-2   Paperback: 478 pages

Design and implement Citrix farms based on XenApp 6.5

1. Use Citrix management tools to publish applications and resources on client devices with this book and eBook.

2. Deploy and optimize XenApp 6.5 on Citrix XenServer, VMware ESX, and Microsoft Hyper-V virtual machines and physical servers.

3. Clear, easy-to-follow steps and screenshots to carry out each task.

www.ingramcontent.com/pod-product-compliance
Lightning Source LLC
Chambersburg PA
CBHW060600060326
40690CB00017B/3781